Education in the Asia-Pacific Region: Issues, Concerns and Prospects

Volume 53

Chong-Jae Lee
Korean Educational Development Institute (KEDI), Seoul, Korea (Republic of)

Naing Yee Mar
GIZ, Yangon, Myanmar

Geoff Masters
Australian Council for Educational Research, Melbourne, Australia

Margarita Pavlova
The Education University of Hong Kong, Hong Kong, China

Max Walsh
Secondary Education Project, Manila, Philippines

Uchita de Zoysa
Global Sustainability Solutions (GLOSS), Colombo, Sri Lanka

The purpose of this Series is to meet the needs of those interested in an in-depth analysis of current developments in education and schooling in the vast and diverse Asia-Pacific Region. The Series will be invaluable for educational researchers, policy makers and practitioners, who want to better understand the major issues, concerns and prospects regarding educational developments in the Asia-Pacific region.

The Series complements the Handbook of Educational Research in the Asia-Pacific Region, with the elaboration of specific topics, themes and case studies in greater breadth and depth than is possible in the Handbook.

Topics to be covered in the Series include: secondary education reform; reorientation of primary education to achieve education for all; re-engineering education for change; the arts in education; evaluation and assessment; the moral curriculum and values education; technical and vocational education for the world of work; teachers and teaching in society; organisation and management of education; education in rural and remote areas; and, education of the disadvantaged.

Although specifically focusing on major educational innovations for development in the Asia-Pacific region, the Series is directed at an international audience.

The Series Education in the Asia-Pacific Region: Issues, Concerns and Prospects, and the Handbook of Educational Research in the Asia-Pacific Region, are both publications of the Asia-Pacific Educational Research Association.

Those interested in obtaining more information about the Monograph Series, or who wish to explore the possibility of contributing a manuscript, should (in the first instance) contact the publishers.

Please contact Melody Zhang (e-mail: melodymiao.zhang@springer.com) for submitting book proposals for this series.

More information about this series at http://www.springer.com/series/5888

Baoyan Cheng • Le Lin • Aiai Fan

The New Journey to the West

Chinese Students' International Mobility

Baoyan Cheng
Department of Educational Foundations
College of Education
University of Hawaii
Honolulu, HI, USA

Le Lin
Department of Sociology
University of Hawaii
Honolulu, HI, USA

Aiai Fan
Graduate School of Education/Institute of
Economics of Education
Peking University
Beijing, China

ISSN 1573-5397　　　　　　　ISSN 2214-9791　(electronic)
Education in the Asia-Pacific Region: Issues, Concerns and Prospects
ISBN 978-981-15-5587-9　　　ISBN 978-981-15-5588-6　(eBook)
https://doi.org/10.1007/978-981-15-5588-6

This Springer imprint is published by the registered company Springer Nature Singapore Pte Ltd.
The registered company address is: 152 Beach Road, #21-01/04 Gateway East, Singapore 189721, Singapore

Series Editors Introduction

This highly informative book by Baoyan Cheng, Le Lin, and Aiai Fan, entitled *The New Journey to the West: Patterns of Chinese Students' International Mobility*, is the latest book to be published in the long-standing Springer Book Series *Education in the Asia-Pacific Region: Issues, Concerns, and Prospects*. The first volume in this Springer series was published in 2002, this book by Cheng, Lin, and Fan being the 53rd volume to be published to date.

A dominant feature of the past several decades, and particularly the first two decades of the twenty-first century, has been the growing importance and all-pervasive impact of globalization. In education, this has involved an increasing mobility of students between countries, and the internationalization of education institutions. This internationalization is expressed through such matters as the expansion of student and faculty exchange programs between universities, the offering of joint degree programs between higher education institutions in different countries, and twinning arrangements between education institutions internationally.

In the case of China, much of this international mobility has focused on the United States and on OECD countries. In the case of the United States, for example, the flow of Chinese students is such that they currently represent 33% of foreign students, followed by India (18%), South Korea (5%), Saudi Arabia (4%), and Canada (2%). In recent years, Australia has become an increasingly popular destination for Chinese students.

This book reports on data obtained through large-scale surveys, and from in-depth interviews. Concerning the international movement of students, particularly in the area of higher education, the book examines the benefits this brings both China and recipient countries, in terms of individuals, the business sector, and civil society, as well as possible negative impacts. Based on the data reported, the authors provide recommendations for students, schools and teachers, parents and school councillors. The book examines the push and full factors for foreign Chinese students; and the impact of international student mobility in financial, cultural, and political terms.

The authors examine and analyze the main drivers behind international student mobility. In doing so, the conceptual framework used is Bourdieu's (1986) frameworks of social and cultural capital, which provides the lenses through which an in-depth analysis of the trends behind international student mobility can be systematically and individually studied.

In terms of the Springer Book Series in which this volume is published, the various topics dealt with in the series are wide ranging and varied in coverage, with an emphasis on cutting-edge developments, best practices, and education innovations for development. Topics examined in the series include: environmental education and education for sustainable development; the interaction between technology and education; the reform of primary, secondary, and teacher education; innovative approaches to education assessment; alternative education; most effective ways to achieve quality and highly relevant education for all; active aging through active learning; case studies of education and schooling in various countries in the region; cross-country and cross-cultural studies of education and schooling; and the sociology of teachers as an occupational group, to mention just a few. More information about the book series is available at http://www.springer.com/series/5888.

All volumes in this series aim to meet the interests and priorities of a diverse education audience including researchers, policy-makers, and practitioners; tertiary students; teachers at all levels within education systems; and members of the public who are interested in better understanding cutting-edge developments in education and schooling in Asia-Pacific.

The main reason why this series has been devoted exclusively to examining various aspects of education and schooling in the Asia-Pacific region is that this is a particularly challenging region. It is renowned for its size, diversity, and complexity, whether it be geographical, socioeconomic, cultural, political, or developmental. Education and schooling in countries throughout the region impact on every aspect of people's lives, including employment, labor force considerations, education and training, cultural orientation, and attitudes and values. Asia and the Pacific is home to some 63% of the world's population of 7 Billion. Countries with the largest populations (China, 1.4 Billion; India, 1.3 Billion) and the most rapidly growing megacities are to be found in the region, as are countries with relatively small populations (Bhutan, 755,000; the island of Niue, 1600).

Levels of economic and sociopolitical development vary widely, with some of the richest countries (such as Japan) and some of the poorest countries on earth (such as Bangladesh). Asia contains the largest number of poor of any region in the world, the incidence of those living below the poverty line remaining as high as 40% in some countries in Asia. At the same time, many countries in Asia are experiencing a period of great economic growth and social development. However, inclusive growth remains elusive, as does growth that is sustainable and does not destroy the quality of the environment. The growing prominence of Asian economies and corporations, together with globalization and technological innovation, are leading to long-term changes in trade, business, and labor markets, to the sociology of populations within (and between) countries. There is a rebalancing of power, centered on Asia and the Pacific region, with the Asian Development Bank in Manila declaring that the twenty-first century will be "the Century of Asia-Pacific."

We believe this book series makes a useful contribution to knowledge sharing about education and schooling in Asia-Pacific.

Any readers of this or other volumes in the series who have an idea for writing their own book (or editing a book) on any aspect of education and/or schooling, that is relevant to the region, are enthusiastically encouraged to approach the series editors either direct or through Springer to publish their own volume in the series since we are always willing to assist perspective authors shape their manuscripts in ways that make them suitable for publication.

School of Education, RMIT University   Rupert Maclean
Melbourne, VIC, Australia
College of Education, Zhejiang University   Lorraine Symaco
Hangzhou, China
9 March 2020

Acknowledgments

It is our privilege to acknowledge the people who have made the publication of this book possible. Lawrence Liu at Springer is the one who inspired us to write this book, and we are grateful to him for his confidence in us and his continuous support of our work. We would also like to thank the anonymous reviewers whose invaluable feedback helped to make the book stronger. Our sincere thanks also go to Drs. Rupert Maclean and Lorraine Pe Symaco, the series editors, as well as Nick Melchior, Melody Zhang, and Sophie Li at Springer for their generous guidance and support during the writing and production process. The following colleagues and friends have taken time out of their busy schedule to comment on parts of the manuscript: Drs. Josh Watson, Georgia Sorenson, and Eileen Tamura, as well as George Sabo and Mark McCormick.

Also in line are our sincere thanks to the various institutions and participants involved in the data collection. Thanks to Professor Wang Rong of the China Institute for Educational Finance Research (CIEFR), and the Finance Department and the International Department of the Ministry of Education of China. Thanks to Professor Zhang Surong from Shenzhen Institute of Educational Sciences and Professor Shi Yu from Chengdu Institute of Educational Sciences.

Last but not least, we are deeply indebted to our families whose love and support is the inexhaustible source of aspiration and motivation.

Contents

Chapter 1
Trends, Reasons, and Impacts of International Student Mobility: A Chinese Perspective

Introduction

With the deepening of globalization during the past several decades, educational institutions around the world have been undergoing rapid internationalization. This education internationalization process is reflected in more frequent student and faculty exchange, more cross-region collaborations in joint-degree programs and branch campuses, as well as "importing foreign higher education services and exporting educational programmes abroad" on a larger scale (Huang, 2007, p. 58). Nowhere is this trend of internalization more apparent than the increased cross-border student mobility.

International student mobility, which refers to "international students … taking a full degree abroad or … participating in a short-term, semester or year-abroad program" (Knight, 2012, p. 24) has become an increasingly important part of the global higher education landscape. Between 1990 and 2012, the number of students studying outside their country of citizenship more than tripled (OECD, 2014). The International Consultants for Education and Fairs (2015) reported that approximately five million students studied abroad in 2014, and that, according to the projection made by OECD, there would be eight million students studying abroad by the year 2025. As Jane Knight claims: "[international] student mobility, in its multiplicity of forms, continues to be a high priority of internationalization" (2012, p. 21).

However, in recent years, there have been trends of decline in international student enrollment. *Open Doors 2018* reports that the enrollment of new international students has dropped for three consecutive years since 2015 (Institute of International Education, 2018). Behind this decline in international student mobility are a series of anti-globalization movements and events in some countries to reassert national identities. These movements and events, such as the impending British exit from the European

© Springer Nature Singapore Pte Ltd. 2020
B. Cheng et al., *The New Journey to the West*, Education in the Asia-Pacific
Region: Issues, Concerns and Prospects 53,
https://doi.org/10.1007/978-981-15-5588-6_1

Union, President Donald Trump's "America first" policies, and the ongoing trade war between the United States and China, have fueled tensions and conflicts among nation states and regions, adding uncertainties to the internationalization of education.

Defining International Student

The term "international student" may seem straightforward at first sight; however, on a closer examination, there may be more complexity to it. Some universities define international students in a practical and functional way. For example, Louisiana State University defines international student as "a non-immigrant student on F-1 or J-1 visa" (as quoted in Kelly, 2012, p. 5). The Organization for Economic Co-operation and Development (OECD)[1] defines international students as "those students who leave their country of origin and move to another country for the purpose of study" (OECD, 2014, p. 79). The United Nations Educational, Scientific, and Cultural Organization (UNESCO) Institute for Statistics defines international students as "those who study in a foreign country of which they are not a permanent resident" (2009, p. 35). In other words, the OECD definition includes permanent residents while the UNESCO one does not. The Institute of International Education (IIE) has changed its definition of international students over time:

> Prior to the 1966–67 survey, a foreign student was defined as a citizen of a country other than the United States, enrolled in an institution of higher education, who intended to return to the home country upon termination of the course of study. Beginning in 1966, the IIE adopted a new definition of foreign student that included all foreign nationals fully enrolled at recognized institutions of higher learning regardless of their visa classification or stated intentions to stay. Beginning with the 1974 survey, the definition was changed again to include only nonimmigrant students (Agarwal & Winkler, 1985, p. 517).

The latest definition used by IIE is more thorough and closer to the definition given by UNESCO: "anyone who is enrolled at an institution of higher education in the United States who is not a US citizen, an immigrant (permanent resident) or a refugee" (as quoted in Kelly, 2012, p. 5). Therefore, one has to be mindful of the diversity in definitions when reading reports prepared by different institutions.

International students crossing national borders are dramatically shaping the cultural, economic, political, and power landscape of the new world order. The Chinese experience offers a particularly enlightening lens into that new order. Drawing on the experience of Chinese students, this chapter provides an overview of international student mobility, with a focus on its trends, reasons, and impacts.

---

[1]Established in 1961 and headquartered in Paris, OECD aims to "promote policies that will improve the economic and social well-being of people around the world." Today, it has 35 members which include many of the world's most advanced countries but also emerging countries like Mexico, Chile, and Turkey (information taken from the OECD website: http://www.oecd.org/about/).

Trends of International Student Mobility

The Uneven Flow of International Students Worldwide

Among the 3.7 million international students who are enrolled at the tertiary level in OECD countries, 56% are from Asia (OECD, 2019). As the largest sending country of international students in the world, China witnessed 662,100 students study abroad in 2018 alone. This number is an increase of 8.83% over the previous year (Ministry of Education, 2019). Between the late 1970s, when China sent out the first dispatch of students overseas after decades of national isolation, and the end of 2015, the total number of Chinese students studying overseas had reached 4.04 million with an average yearly growth rate of 19.06% for nearly four decades (Ministry of Education, 2016). In other words, even though the growth rate of overseas Chinese students has dropped in recent years, the general trend has been upward. On the receiving side, Australia, Canada, the United Kingdom and the United States together hosted more than 40% of the mobile students who studied in OECD and partner countries (OECD, 2019).

The flow direction of international students is mostly from developing, non-English-speaking countries in the East such as China and India to developed, English-speaking countries in the West such as the United States, the United Kingdom, and Australia. According to Perkins and Neumayer (2014), in 2009, the flow of international students from developing to developed countries accounted for 56% of the global total number of mobile students whereas the flow in the other direction only accounted for 0.9%. The other flows were from developed to developed countries (24.6%) and from developing to developing countries (18.3%).

The Flow of Chinese Students to the United States

The largest flow of international students, among the uneven flows worldwide, is from China to the United States. China was the top sending country of international students to the United States in the 1990s and has surpassed India and once again become the top sending country since 2009. The United States has also been the most popular destination for Chinese students in recent decades. In 2017, close to 1.1 million international students enrolled in American colleges and universities, and 363,341 (about 33%) of them were Chinese (Institute of International Education, 2018).

China-US educational exchanges date back to the nineteenth century. *Yung Wing* (also spelled as *Rong Hong*, or *Jung Hung*), who is considered the father of China's study-abroad movement in the modern era, came to the United States in 1847 at the age of 19. After finishing 3 years of study at the Monson Academy in Massachusetts, he was enrolled at Yale University in 1850. Upon graduating from Yale in 1854, he returned to China immediately in spite of superior job opportunities in the United States. While studying at Yale, he realized that "the rising generation of China should enjoy the same educational advantage that I had enjoyed; that through western education China may be regenerated" (Chu, 2004, p. 7). Thanks to his persevering efforts in convincing the Qing imperial government to send students abroad, the Qing government sent its first dispatch of 30 teenage students to the United States in 1872. For each of the following three consecutive years, another 30 teenage students were sent, making it a total of 120 between 1872 and 1875. This series of state-led action marks the beginning of Chinese students studying overseas on a relatively large scale. We will provide a detailed account of this historical background in Chap. 2 of this book.

Over the next one hundred years or so, China and the United States engaged in intermittent educational exchanges. During the first half of the twentieth century, educational exchanges between the two countries expanded rapidly, and China had sent more students and scholars to the United States than to any other country during the first four decades (Li, 2008). However, this exchange was put to a full stop in the early 1950s due to the breakout of the Korean War. It was not until after 1978, when China opened its door to the outside world after almost three decades of closure, that educational exchange between the two countries resumed. On December 26, 1978, a group of 50 Chinese scholars and scientists, funded by the Chinese government, left for the United States. This marked the beginning of an increasingly active exchange relationship between the United States and China for years to come.

As shown in Table 1.1, the number of Chinese students studying in the United States rose from 59,939 in 2000 to 304,040 in 2014, representing an increase of over 400%. The increase rate has accelerated since 2007, and in 2014–2015 the number of Chinese students studying in the United States increased by 10.8% over the previous year. The year of 2014–2015 also marks the eighth consecutive year of double-digit growth. Since then, however, the growth rate has decreased to 8.1, 6.8, and 3.6% for 2015–2016, 2016–2017, and 2017–2018, respectively. As shown in Table 1.2, among the top five countries of origin in 2017–2018 (namely, China, India, South Korea, Saudi Arabia, and Canada), Chinese students accounted for 33.2% of

Table 1.1 Number of Chinese students in the United States (2000–2014)

Year	2000–2001	2001–2002	2003–2004	2005–2006	2007–2008	2009–2010	2011–2012	2013–2014	2014–2015
Number (rank)	59,939 (1)	63,211 (2)	61,765 (2)	62,582 (2)	81,127 (2)	127,628 (1)	194,029 (1)	274,439 (1)	304,040 (1)
% of all international students	10.9	10.8	10.8	11.1	13.0	18.5	25.4	31	31
% change over previous year	10.0	5.5	−4.6	0.1	19.8	29.9	23.1	16.5	10.8

Source: Compiled from Institute of International Education (2000–2015). *Open doors*

Table 1.2 Top places of origin of international students in the United States (2017–2018)

Rank	Place of origin	2017/2018	% of total	% of change
1	China	363,341	33.2	3.6
2	India	196,271	17.9	5.4
3	South Korea	54,555	5.0	−7.0
4	Saudi Arabia	44,432	4.1	−15.5
5	Canada	25,909	2.4	−4.3

Source: Institute of International Education (2018). *Open doors 2018*

all international students studying in the Unites States. This percentage was higher than that of the other four countries combined.

One noticeable trend is the increasingly young age of Chinese students studying overseas. Among Chinese students studying in the United States, the percentage of undergraduate Chinese students has been growing rapidly and steadily. In 2005–2006, only 14.9% of Chinese students studied at the undergraduate level, and 76.1% at the graduate level. In 2013–2014, the percentage of undergraduate students reached 40.3 while the percentage for graduate students dropped to 42.1. In 2014–2015, the percentage of undergraduate students (41%) surpassed that of graduate students (39.6%) for the first time. Accompanying the increase in the percentage of undergraduate Chinese students in the United States has been a steady decrease in the average age of Chinese students over the years. In fact, an increasing number of Chinese high school students has entered the United States: in 2009 China surpassed South Korean and became the No. 1 sending country of international high school students in the United States. In 2005–2006, only 65 Chinese students came to the United States to attend high school, whereas in 2013, Chinese students accounted for 46% of the 49,000 international students seeking US high school diplomas (Farrugia, 2014). In 2016, the total number of Chinese students studying in American K-12 schools rose to 35,627 (Lew, 2016).

"Parachute Kids": An Asian Phenomenon

An important contribution this book makes is its inclusion of young Chinese students studying overseas at the secondary level. Those students are often called "parachute kids," a term education researchers used to describe "unaccompanied minors" (Popadiuk, 2009, p. 230), "unaccompanied sojourners" (Kuo & Roysircar, 2006, p. 161), or "little overseas students" (Tsong & Liu, 2009, p. 366) from Asian regions such as Taiwan, Hong Kong, South Korea, Malaysia, Indonesia, and mainland China. Very often these students are dropped off in the United States to go to school while their parents stay in their country of origin (Fu, 1994). Parachute kids first emerged in the 1980s, and during the 1980s and early 1990s, the parachute kids phenomenon gained increased media attention partly because parachute kids were predominently from Taiwan (Hamilton, 1993; Zhou, 1998). There was also an upsurge of parachute kids from Hong Kong in the 1990s. These parachute kids from Taiwan and Hong Kong, typically between eight and 18 years old, attended elementary, middle or high school in the United States. They usually stay with family friends or relatives, or live in home-stay arrangements where a host family serves as the paid caretaker (Hsieh, 2007). Families of parachute kids are also known as "astronaut families" or gireogi gah-jok (goose) families in Korean because the parents have to fly frequently between Asia and the United States (Shih, 2016). The reasons for parachuting include the opportunities for better education in destination countries and fierce competition for limited educational resources at home. Although the term "parachute kids" originally refers to overseas students without the company of their parents, increasingly this term has been used interchangeably with "little overseas students." After all, most of the young overseas students do study abroad on their own, regardless of whether their parents provide onsite care. In this book, the term "parachute kids" is used to refer to the young overseas student population at the secondary level.

Although a large number of these children in the 1980s and 1990s came from Taiwan and Hong Kong, parachute kids from other Asian countries started to gain increased attention in the 2000s. For example, Kang and Abelmann (2011) pointed out that pre-college overseas studies experienced a dramatic increase in the mid-2000s among South Korean students. Compared to parachute kids from Taiwan who tend to come from wealthy and often entrepreneurial families, parachute kids from South Korea represent a wider socioeconomic range (Lee & Friedlander, 2014).

During the past decade, the number of parachute kids from mainland China has been rapidly rising. Interestingly, media portrayals of the parachute kids tend to focus on the "nouveau riche" aspect of those students, such as their squandering of money, spending behaviors and academic unpreparedness (Huang, 2016; Liu, 2015).[2] Indeed, Chinese students who have been studying overseas in recent years are very different from their predecessors who embarked on the same journey two decades earlier. An article in *Foreign Policy* (Liu, 2015) depicts typical Chinese students studying overseas in the 1980s and 1990s this way: They tended to be among "the nation's best and brightest"; they are usually "... penniless ... didn't go out to dinner, didn't go to parties, and assumed that American students were all really rich" and they tended to be "idealistic and patriotic." In less than two decades, the image of humble and diligent overseas Chinese students has transformed drastically and is replaced by the image of the "nouveau riche," or "the second-generation scion in a wealthy family, who studies abroad in order to return home to run the family business." They "pay full tuition, often study finance, business management, or economics, and spend their time clustered together"; and they drive luxury cars and go into the city "for extravagant weekend shopping trips" (ibid).

---

[2] For more reports on Chinese students showing off their wealth, please refer to Higgins (2013) on *Bloomberg*, and Drash (2015) on CNN.

Where Do International Students Go and Why

Push and Pull Factors

The push-and-pull framework has been one of the most widely used theories for guiding migration studies for many years (Ravenstein, 1885; Stouffer, 1940). Everett S. Lee is the one who develops the framework into a model, as shown in Fig. 1.1. Donald Bogue (1969), one of the leading demographers in the United States, enriches the model by identifying specific push-and-pull factors. Many researchers have further enriched the model (Agarwal & Winkler, 1985; Altbach, 1991; Mazzarol, Kemp, & Savery, 1997; Mazzarol & Soutar, 2002; McMahon, 1992).

An improved approach to the basic push-and-pull framework involves distinguishing four groups of factors: (1) push factors in home countries and (2) pull factors in host countries, both of which motivate students to leave their home countries, as well as (3) pull factors in home countries and (4) push factors in host countries, both of which prevent students from leaving their home countries. Tan (2013) regroups the four factors as the following: (1) domestic push factors, (2) external push factors, (3) domestic pull factors, and (4) external pull factors. Students leave their home countries to pursue study in another country when the pushing force exceeds the pulling force. We will provide a more comprehensive review of the push-and-pull framework in Chap. 4. We will further identify the inadequacy of this framework and suggest directions for its improvement in Chaps. 5 and 8.

Push-and-Pull Factors for Chinese Students

Educational researchers have implemented the push-and-pull framework to understand Chinese students' motives to study abroad or stay in China. For example, Li and Bray (2007) call the pull factors in home countries and push factors in host countries "reverse push-pull factors" (p. 795). They identify the following reverse pull factors that tend to keep Chinese students from studying abroad: a desire to stay with one's family, awareness of the relevance of domestic education, and increasing internationalization of domestic institutions. They also identify the following reverse

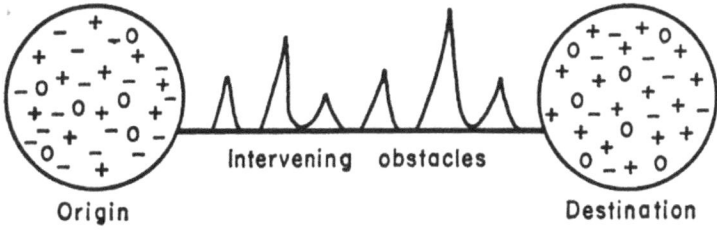

Origin   Intervening obstacles   Destination

Fig. 1.1 Origin and destination factors and intervening obstacles in migration. (Source: Everett S. Lee, "A Theory of Migration," *Demography*, 3 (1966), p. 48)

push factors of host countries which discourage Chinese students from overseas studies: increasing fees and other costs for higher education, restrictive policies on foreign students and tightening of immigration policies. To further develop the push-and-pull factor framework, Li and Bray (2007) propose to use four categories of motives: academic, economic, social and cultural, and political:

Academic motives include pursuit of qualifications and professional development; economic motives include access to scholarships, estimated economic returns from study, and prospects for employment; social and cultural factors include a desire to obtain experience and understanding of other societies; and political motives embraced such factors as commitment to society and enhancement of political status and power (p. 795).

For each aforementioned category, push factors in China and pull factors in host countries work together to enable the international mobility of Chinese students. Academically, educational opportunity and educational quality are the most significant factors. First, intense competition in China is an important push factor (Iannelli & Huang, 2014). There has been a rapid expansion of Chinese higher education during the past few decades. College enrollment has steadily risen from 1.66 million in 1980 to 15 million in 2002, with especially substantial increases of 24.31%, 36.78%, and 23.21% for 1999, 2000, and 2001, respectively (Chen, 2002). In 2013, the total enrollment of China's higher education institutions was nearly 36 million (Ministry of Education, 2015), and the enrollment rate among students between the ages of 18 and 22 reached 37.5%, compared to 15% in 2002 and 3.4% in 1990 (Wu & Lu, 2002). Nonetheless, entering a decent college or university is still competitive and the options of entrance are limited. The National College-Entrance Examination is still the main avenue through which students can access higher education. In 2014, 9.98 million students took the examination, and 9.39 million, or 74.3% of them were admitted (Sina Education, 2015).

The second notable push factor is the dissatisfaction of Chinese students and their families with the higher education system in China. For example, the quality of curricula and teaching methods in China's higher education system have been considered by Chinese students as "not as advanced and up-to-date as those adopted by higher education institutions in Western countries" (Iannelli & Huang, 2014, p. 808). Corresponding to these push factors in China are pull factors in host countries, such as world-renowned reputation of higher education institutions and their high quality and flexible programs (Azmat et al., 2013; Iannelli & Huang, 2014; To, Lung, Lai, & Lai, 2014). Third, some efforts made by institutions in host countries may serve to pull Chinese students into those countries. For example, the establishment of foundation courses or access courses in China by institutions such as the Northern Consortium UK, which is composed of 11 universities in the United Kingdom, has helped to provide Chinese students with direct access to UK universities (Iannelli & Huang, 2014).

Economically, the rise of China's economy serves as an indispensable pushing force. Self-sponsored studying overseas used to be a privilege reserved for the few most wealthy and powerful elites in China, but now even many white-collar professionals can afford to send their children abroad. The growing purchase power of these professionals has benefited from improved living standards, accelerated wealth accumulation, skyrocketing real estate price, as well as the overall appreciation of the Chinese currency since the mid-1990s. In spite of the increasing affordability of studying overseas for average Chinese families, its financial cost is still a major consideration for most Chinese families, and thus serves as a push factor in host countries (Azmat et al., 2013). Politically, loosened restrictions on visa and immigration in host countries may serve as a pulling force. Sociocultural factors can serve as both pushing and pulling forces, as demonstrated in existing studies of motivations for mobility among immigrants and international students. For example, Mazzarol and Soutar (2002) listed "the desire to have a better understanding of the Western culture" as a push factor from the home country.

Patterns and Impact of International Student Mobility

Researchers in various disciplines, such as demography, geography, economics and education, have made continuing efforts to gauge the patterns and impact of international student mobility. Some of these scholars have adopted the World System Theory to depict general patterns of the mobility.

Uneven Flow of Students and World System Theory

World System Theory has been used to explain the uneven flow of international students around the world. According to this theory (Wallerstein, 2004), the whole world is a capitalist world-economy system, and countries are divided into three groups based on "the degree of profitability of the production processes" (Wallerstein, 2004, p. 28). These three groups are countries engaged in core-like production processes, countries engaged in peripheral production processes, and semi-peripheral countries that have "a near even mix of core-like and peripheral products" (p. 28). The core countries are developed ones that hold hegemonic political and economic power and they are the origin of products, knowledge, skills, ideology and values. Examples of core countries are the United States and United Kingdom. The peripheral countries are usually underdeveloped ones that receive both physical and ideological products from core countries. Examples of this group include many African and South American countries such as Kenya and Ecuador. Semi-peripheral countries are those between core and peripheral countries and they constantly struggle to move up the hierarchical ladder of world order. Examples of semi-peripheral countries include newly industrialized ones such as China and Brazil. According to the World System Theory, there is an "unequal exchange" between the core and peripheral countries (i.e., strong and weak states) because of the "constant flow of surplus-value from the producers of peripheral products to the producers of core-like products" (p. 28). Furthermore, "[s]trong states relate to weak states by pressuring them to accept cultural practices" such as "educational policy, including where university students may study" (p. 55).

One implication of the World System Theory for international student mobility is that a country's position in the international student exchange network is highly correlated with its economic and political power and influence. Empirical studies have confirmed this argument: when measuring a country's influence in the world system by the country's Gross National Product per capita, scholars found that the higher a country's position is in the world system, the more central it is in the international student exchange network (Barnett & Wu, 1995; Chen & Barnett, 2000). The fact that an increasing number of overseas Chinese students return to China corresponds to China's move to the core in the world system. In 2018, the total number of overseas Chinese students who returned to China was 519,400, whereas 662,100 Chinese students went overseas to study in the same year. By comparison, the number of returned overseas Chinese students was only 9121 in 2000, while 32,000 left China for overseas studies during that year. In fact, the number of overseas students returning to China rose by double-digit in recent years. For example, the rate of growth are 46.6% and 29.5% for 2012 and 2013, respectively. Even though the increasing rate dropped to 11.19% and 8% for 2017 and 2018, respectively, the general trend has been upward during the past years and will likely to sustain for years to come (Center for China and Globalization, 2015a, b; Ministry of Education, 2019; New Oriental, 2015).

Another implication of the World System Theory is that international student exchanges are uneven. There has been more student outflow from peripheral and semi-peripheral countries into core countries than the other way around. Some scholars argue that this uneven flow may reinforce the economic and political inequality among countries, and vice versa (Barnett & Wu, 1995). In other words, the uneven flow and the inequality in world order are likely to persist. This argument, although potentially valid when put to empirical test, may have oversimplified the World System Theory when applying this theory to international student mobility. According to Wallerstein (2004), the world system is not static. It has been changing incrementally over the years and the accumulated change may result in a fundamental shift in world order one day. In addition, periphery and semi-periphery countries are not merely passive recipients of the products from the core countries and the former-group countries have their own agency in moving their positions toward the center. With regard to the international mobility of students, uneven student flow does not necessarily mean loss of talent for a home country. A large number of overseas Chinese students have been making their contributions to the rapid development of China, regardless of whether they have returned to China or not. As Acemoglu (2006) argues, the issue of brain drain has been exaggerated in previous studies. Similarly, Yue (2013) states:

> The returned students and scholars play a leading role in areas like education, science and technology, high-tech industries, finance, insurance, trade and management and serve as a driving force for the country's economic and social development. At the same time, many students and scholars staying abroad contribute in various ways such as giving lectures

during short-term visits to China, having academic exchanges, conducting joint research, bringing in projects and investments and providing information and technical consultancy (p. 27).

Further, the rise of Asia as a popular destination for international students indicates that the uneven flow is subject to changes. According to a report by the Bangkok Office of UNESCO, the dominance of the United States, the United Kingdom, and Australia in the network of student mobility met a challenge as early as the mid-1990s. By the early 2010s, some Asian countries such as China, Singapore, and Malaysia had become competitive destinations for foreign students (Tan, 2013, p. 1).

The changing world system prompts us to rethink the categorization of host countries that was previously theorized under the core-periphery framework. Lasanowaski (2009) divides host countries into four categories based on their share in serving international students worldwide. The first group includes the three "major players", namely, the United States, the United Kingdom, and Australia. They host around half of all international students worldwide. The second group are the "middle powers" which together host around a quarter of all international students. Countries belonging to this group include Germany, France, and China. The third group is the "shape shifters" which account for around 10% of the world's overseas students: Canada, New Zealand, and Japan. The fourth group includes the "emerging contenders" which account for more than 5% of the total international student mobility. Countries in this group are Singapore, Malaysia, and South Korea, and they mostly host the inflow of students from Asian countries. The position of China and the role of the fourth group in this categorization once again substantiate the increasing importance of Asian countries as destinations of international student mobility.

Economic Impact and the Human Capital Framework

It is widely recognized that receiving and educating international students benefit host countries in multiple ways. As Rogers (1984) notes: "there is a consensus that the presence of foreign students enriches intellectual, cultural and social life" (p. 21). Victor Johnson (2003), a former Associate Executive Director for public policy at NAFSA: Association of International Educators, also acknowledges various benefits international students bring to the United States. These benefits include adding diversity to the student body, providing American students with the first close contact with another culture, filling the under-enrolled science courses and providing crucial academic support by hiring international students as teaching and research assistants. Sir Richard Sykes, a former rector of Imperial College London where a third of undergraduates and about half of postgraduates come from outside Britain, attributes the improvement of academic climate to the presence of large numbers of Chinese students. "The Chinese work bloody hard and drive up the standards," he says, and "other students see that, and they have to compete" (The Economist, 2010).

Another major rationale for recruiting international students among higher education institutions in host countries is economic benefits. In the majority of countries where data are available, international students pay higher tuition fees at public educational institutions than do domestic students enrolled in the same institutions. As American higher education institutions faced an increasingly restrained budget situation after the 2008 financial crisis, many of them turn to the vast Chinese market for a solution. Let us offer a few examples. In 2011, Zinch China, a consulting company that provides service to American colleges and universities, was asked by the provost of a large American university to help recruit 250 Chinese students in order to fill the university's budget deficit (Bartlett & Fischer, 2011). Another example involves the University of Delaware, where the majority of international students are from China. In the 2011–2012 academic year, the number of Chinese students at this institution reached 517, whereas this number was only 8 in 2007. In order to address its budget challenges, Oklahoma Christian University has also drastically increased the number of international students from China. This university started recruiting international students in 2007, and a quarter of its current 250 international students came from China.

Since international students are considered an important revenue source, it is no surprise that studies have been conducted to estimate the costs and benefits of international students to local economies. These studies typically employ the human capital framework to estimate the costs and benefits (e.g., Throsby, 1999).

One of the earlier efforts in estimating the economic impact was made by Gruebel and Scott (1966). Their estimates of costs include direct education cost, maintenance cost, and transportation cost. Chishti (1984) includes in his estimates such costs as educational and general expenditures, user cost of capital, and various indirect costs such as maintenance costs of foreign students who receive their allowance from US sources. Benefits included in his estimates are tuition revenue and contribution to aggregate demand because foreign students consume goods and services during their stay in the United States. Moreover, he uses the cost of producing equivalent human capital in host country to estimate the value of embodied capital in non-returnees. He concludes that even though tuition paid by foreign students only covers about 37% of the cost of their education in the United States, benefits for the United States outweigh costs in educating foreign students because there are substantial indirect benefits in terms of human capital gains.

Many other studies analyze direct and indirect costs and benefits at the local, regional, and national levels (Throsby, 1991). The report *The Economic Costs and Benefits of International Students*, which was produced by the Oxford Economics in 2013, quantifies the costs and benefits of international students in Sheffield to the local economy. Both costs and benefits are divided into three categories, namely, direct (which refers to the economic activity resulting from the direct presence of international students at university), indirect (which consists of activity that is supported as a result of local supply-chain purchases, the additional local procurement resulting from these purchases and so on), and induced (which involves activity that is supported by the spending of those employed as a result of direct and indirect impacts).This report further shows how UK and multiple regions within UK have benefited from educating international students.

Description of the Book

Largely based on data collected through large-scale survey, organization archives and in-depth interviews over the years, this book provides a comprehensive examination of the cross-border mobility of Chinese students. We addresses the questions of *which* Chinese social groups intend to study overseas, *why* they want to study overseas, *what* the impacts of the mobility are on China's social stratification, and *what* the challenges are in those students' adaptation to their lives in destination countries. In this book, Chinese students' international mobility is examined from both ends, namely, the sending end (i.e., China) and the destination end (e.g., America).

Chapter 2 of the book provides a historical perspective on the international mobility of Chinese students by examining the experiences of *Yung Wing*, the "father of overseas Chinese students," and the subsequent two waves of Chinese students going overseas to study in modern history. The first wave includes the 120 "fortunate sons" who studied in the United States between 1872 and 1881; the second wave includes Chinese students going to Japan to study after 1895, and those studying in America on the Boxer Indemnity Scholarship between 1909 and 1940. A common theme runs through this nearly 200-year history of Chinese students studying overseas: How can China become a modern nation capable of competing with the West on the international scene? The high hopes placed upon those students made them susceptible to criticisms and caused the public perceptions of them to pendulate between patriots and traitors, heroes and villains, and vanguard and scapegoat, even though they had paved the way for China's modernization. This chapter not only presents factual information on those major historical figures and events relevant to studying overseas, but also provides analysis on the impacts of those events on individuals involved as well as the Chinese society at large.

Chapter 3 describes contemporary China and its education system as the context for the international mobility of Chinese students. It presents an overview of the contemporary Chinese society and education system, including the system's strengths and weaknesses, especially the key characteristic of examination culture. This chapter also provides information on the internationalization of secondary schools in China, especially international programs in key high schools and the increasing popularity of international schools.

Chapters 4 and 5 address the question of which Chinese social group wants to study overseas and why, with the former chapter focusing on quantitative data and latter on in-depth case studies. Applying the push-and-pull framework and using data on 3001 students at 18 high schools located in three Chinese cities, Chap. 4 depicts a comprehensive picture of the Chinese students who intend to study overseas. Extending the quantitative patterns outlined in Chap. 4 and drawing on in-depth interview data, Chap. 5 presents rich stories of three Chinese students who currently study or work in the US. This chapter also makes suggestions for further developing the push-and-pull framework.

Chapter 6 addresses the question of what impacts international student mobility may have on the Chinese society, especially on its social stratification. Through analyzing original survey data from 1,012 ninth graders at 9 middle schools collected in Beijing in 2015, this chapter examines the differential in the choice of and access to such educational resources as studying overseas among different social strata in China. Particular attention is paid to students from those groups which are at an advantage in building networks and mobilizing social resources, namely, high-ranking officials, wealthy business owners, and white-collar professionals. By ana-lyzing how different social strata differ in their willingness and plan to study overseas, this empirical study has shown that studying overseas, which is considered an option for pursuing high-quality educational resources, has proven to be such a tool for advantaged social classes to maintain their status and for disadvantaged social classes to climb up the social ladder.

Chapter 7 examines Chinese students studying overseas from the destination-country side. Based on a research project which collected data through interviews with 15 Chinese students enrolled at a private American high school and 7 teachers who have worked with them, this chapter presents stories of 3 "parachute kids" as in-depth case studies. Those stories demonstrate the challenges they face in the sociocultural adaptation process because of language barrier, emotional problems, and discipline issues, as well as their lack of bonding with parents.

Chapter 8 investigates the education and training industry that provides supplemental education services on study-abroad-related tests, such as Test of English as a Foreign Language (TOEFL), Graduate Record Examination (GRE), Scholastic Aptitude Test (SAT), and International English Language Testing System (IELTS). Breaking away from existing paradigms that either examines the demand or the supply side of overseas studies, this chapter puts the spotlight on test-preparation schools as the "visible hands" behind the ever-growing study-abroad waves in China. This chapter first introduces the social context, development trajectory of this industry and how multiple local niche markets evolved into an integrated industry. Then, this chapter illustrates how these test-preparation schools helped Chinese students acquire indispensable information regarding how to crack the tests and apply for overseas schools. Chapter 8 further shows the ways in which test-preparation schools instilled in students the meaning of study-abroad and boosted the motivation and demand of overseas studies.

Chapter 9 calls on attention to the potential transformational effect of international sojourning experiences. While running the risk of increasing global inequality, transnational mobility provides opportunities for students to build solidarity with each other and instill in them a cosmopolitan spirit.

Concluding Remarks

In studying the main drives behind international student mobility, a mere examination of the political and economic factors is insufficient; the social and cultural factors also have to be taken into consideration. Here, Bourdieu's frameworks of social and cultural capital can provide the lenses through which we can discern the systematic trends behind international student mobility. Bourdieu (1986) divided capital into three categories: (1) economic capital, "which is immediately and directly convertible into money and may be institutionalized in the form of property rights" (p. 243), (2) cultural capital, which can exist in three forms, namely, "the embodied state" (i.e., culture and cultivation), "the objectified state" (i.e., material objects and media, such as writings, paintings, monuments, and instruments), and "the institutionalized state" (i.e., institutional recognition such as academic qualifications), and (3) social capital, which refers to "the aggregate of the actual or potential resources which are linked to possession of a durable network of more or less institutionalized relationships of mutual acquaintance and recognition … which provides each of its members with the backing of the collectivity-owned capital" (pp. 248–249). Bourdieu further notes that cultural and social capital are convertible to economic capital under certain conditions. Cultural and social capital are highly relevant and appropriate for the study of international student mobility because of the central role of academic qualifications and educational credentials in the mobility process.

Bourdieu (1986)'s theory of capital can be used to unravel the multiplicity of benefits associated with overseas studies. The identified benefits include gains in human capital, which refers to knowledge and skills, as well as social capital, which refers to the network and relationships established overseas, and lastly, cultural capital, which refers to enriched multi-cultural life experiences and global perspective. As Agarwal and Winkler (1985) summarize:

> These benefits include the quality of instruction and research, higher expected lifetime income, the prestige of a foreign degree (especially a graduate degree from an American university), and international contacts that may facilitate future business dealings, travel, or research. In addition, there are the benefits of living in another culture during a student's educational experience (p. 514).

In fact, in addition to examining the migration of students across countries or regions from a human capital perspective—which implies that going to another country to study is considered an investment and the motive is to have better job opportunities and thus higher expected income in the future—cross-border migration of international students may also be viewed as a consumption choice. In that case, students not only consider the returns to their educational investment, they also consider the circumstances and the place where they will study (Beine, Noel, & Ragot, 2013).

In addition, studies of international student mobility need to look at both the benefits and the potential negative impacts of mobility. Globalization can be a double-edged sword. On the one hand, it could potentially make the world flat (or less uneven) by providing opportunities for all countries to participate in economic activities, thanks to advancement in technology and communications. Asia seems to be the main beneficiary of globalization. Asian countries and regions that have benefited include China and the "Four Little Tigers" of Hong Kong, Singapore, South Korea, and Taiwan. On the other hand, globalization can increase inequality—both within countries and among countries, and weakens cultural diversity, as demonstrated by the stagnant development of Latin American countries and worsened situation of African countries.

Stiglitz (2006) confirms this controversial role of globalization by conducting a systematic comparison between Latin American and African countries on one hand and Asian countries on the other hand. He demonstrates that Latin American countries have been harmed by the Washington Consensus and African countries have been bypassed by globalization due to their colonial heritage, lack of infrastructure, and the AIDS epidemic. In contrast, Asia has managed to make globalization work for them mainly because of their strong governments. Despite being one of the major beneficiaries of globalization, China has paid enormous price: environmental destruction, exploitation of labor, and loss of traditional values/lifestyle to some extent.

This book also calls for closer scrutiny of other controversial issues in international student mobility. These issues include, but are not limited to, diploma mill, phony universities, and the use of educational agencies for recruiting international students. An example of diploma mill is Dickson State University in North Dakota which awarded 4-year degrees to 400 international students who did not fulfill all the graduate requirements (Fischer, 2012).

Another example of this kind involves fraud and crime. In November 2014, Susan Xiao-Ping Su, president and chief executive of Tri-Valley University, was sentenced to 16 years in prison for student-visa fraud, harboring undocumented immigrants and other charges. Federal agents raided this California-based institution in January 2011 because of complaints accusing the university of admitting international students so that they could stay in the United States on student visas while not having to attend classes (U.S. Immigration and Customs Enforcement, 2014). Even worse, a 2011 *Chronicle of Higher Education* investigative report suggested that Tri-Valley University was only the tip of the iceberg, and similar unaccredited institutions, which exploit loopholes in visa to make money off international students, flourish in states such as California and Virginia where regulations are lax (Bartlett & Fischer, 2011).

International student mobility, like globalization, can be a double-edged sword. On the one hand, as part of the worldwide population migration, cross-border mobility among students is affected by the world order and its political and economic forces. This indicates that inequalities among countries may be further increased by the uneven flow of international students, and "brain drain" remains a bleak reality for many developing countries. On the other hand, as a unique kind of population migration, international student mobility can exert influence on the world order due to the transformational function of education and the agency within each individual. Countries are often proactive in making the inflow and outflow of students work in their favor.

References

Acemoglu, D. (2006). Economic inequality and globalization. *Brown Journal of World Affairs, 13*(1), 19–27.

Agarwal, V. B., & Winkler, D. R. (1985). Migration of foreign students to the United States. *The Journal of Higher Education, 56*(5), 509–522.

Altbach, P. G. (1991). Impact and adjustment: Foreign students in comparative perspective. *Higher Education, 21*(3), 305–323.

Azmat, F., Osborne, A., Rossignol, K. L., Jogulu, U., Rentschler, R., Robottom, I., et al. (2013). Understanding aspirations and expectations of international students in Australian higher education. *Asia Pacific Journal of Education, 33*(1), 97–111.

Barnett, G. A., & Wu, R. (1995). The international student exchange network: 1970 & 1989. *Higher Education, 30*(4), 353–368.

Bartlett, T., & Fischer, K. (2011, November 3). The China conundrum: American colleges find the Chinese student boon a tricky fit. *The Chronicle of Higher Education*. Retrieved from http://www.chronicle.com/article/The-China-Conundrum/129628

Beine, M., Noel R., & Ragot, L. (2013). *The determinants of international mobility of students.* CEPII working paper.

Bogue, D. J. (1969). *Principles of demography*. New York, NY: John Wiley & Sons.

Bourdieu, P. (1986). The forms of capital. In J. G. Richardson (Ed.), *Handbook of theory and research for the sociology of education* (pp. 241–258). Westport, CT: Greenwood Press.

Center for China and Globalization. (2015a). *Report on China's study abroad*. Beijing: Social Science Academic Press.

Center for China and Globalization. (2015b). *Report on Chinese students returned from overseas.*

Chen, T., & Barnett, G. A. (2000). Research on international student flows from a macro perspective: A network analysis of 1985, 1989 and 1995. *Higher Education, 39*(4), 435–453.

Chen, Z. (2002). Problems in the massification of Chinese higher education and some suggestions. *Journal of Changde Teachers University, 27*(3), 93–95.

Chishti, S. (1984). Economic costs and benefits of educating foreign students in the United States. *Research in Higher Education, 21*(4), 397–414.

Chu, T. K. (2004). 150 years of Chinese students in America. *Harvard China Review, 1*(1), 7–21.

Drash, W. (2015, August 5). Culture clash in Iowa: The town where bubble tea shops outnumber Starbucks. *CNN.*

Farrugia, C. A. (2014). *New pathways to higher education: International secondary students in the United States*. New York, NY: Institute of International Education.

Fischer, K. (2012, February 19). American Colleges' missteps raise questions about overseas partnerships. *Chronicle of Higher Education.*

Fu, N. (1994). Parachute kids and astronaut parents. *Transpacific, 9*(3), 32–39.

Gruebel, H. G., & Scott, A. D. (1966). The cost of U.S. exchange programs. *The Journal of Human Resources, 1*(2), 81–98.

Hamilton, D. (1993, June 24). A house, cash—And no parents. *Los Angeles Times.*

Higgins, T. (2013, December 19). Chinese students major in luxury cars. *Bloomberg.*

Hsieh, P. (2007). *Taiwanese parachute kids: A retrospective qualitative exploration of adults who came to the United States as unaccompanied minors.* Unpublished doctoral dissertation, Alliant International University, San Diego, CA.

Huang, F. (2007). Internationalisation of higher education in the era of globalization: What have been its implications in China and Japan? *Higher Education Management and Policy, 19*(1), 47–57.

Huang, H. (2016, December 21). A "parachute kid" from China dropped out after spending $80,000 and studying at 3 schools within one year. *World Journal.*

Iannelli, C., & Huang, J. (2014). Trends in participation and attainment of Chinese students in UK higher education. *Studies in Higher Education, 39*(5), 805–855.

Institute of International Education. (2000–2015). *Open doors*. New York, NY: Institute of International Education.

Institute of International Education. (2018). *Open doors*. New York, NY: Institute of International Education.

International Consultants for Education, & Fairs, M. (2015). *The state of international student mobility in 2015*. Retrieved from http://monitor.icef.com/2015/11/the-state-of-international-student-mobilityin-2015/website

Johnson, V. (2003). The perils of homeland security: When we hinder foreign students and scholars, we endanger our national security. *The Chronicle of Higher Education, 49*(31), B7.

Kang, J., & Abelmann, N. (2011). The domestication of South Korean pre-college study abroad in the first decade of the millennium. *The Journal of Korean Studies, 16*(1), 89–118.

Kelly, S. S. (2012). *Economic impact of international students attending an institution of higher education in the United States* (Doctoral dissertation, Louisiana State University). Retrieved from http://etd.lsu.edu/docs/available/etd-01202012-124540/unrestricted/Economic_Impact_of_International_Students_S_Kelly.pdf

Knight, J. (2012). Student mobility and internationalization: Trends and tribulations. *Research in Comparative and International Education, 7*(1), 20–33.

Kuo, B. C. H., & Roysircar, G. (2006). An exploratory study of cross-cultural adaptation of adolescent Taiwanese unaccompanied sojourners in Canada. *International Journal of Intercultural Relations, 30*, 159–183.

Lasanowaski, V. (2009). *International student mobility: Status report 2009*. Retrieved from the Observatory on Borderless Higher Education website: http://www.obhe.ac.uk/documents/view_details?id=759

Lee, E. S. (1966). A theory of migration. *Demography, 3*(1), 47–57.

Lee, H., & Friedlander, M. L. (2014). Predicting depressive symptoms from acculturative family distancing: A study of Taiwanese parachute kids in adulthood. *Cultural Diversity and Ethnic Minority Psychology, 20*(3), 458–462.

Lew, T. (2016, October 4). Chinese "parachute kids" tackle U.S. schools on their own. The Hechinger Report. Retrieved from http://hechingerreport.org/chinese-parachute kidstackle-u-s-schools/.

Li, H. (2008). *U.S.-China educational exchange: State, society, and intercultural relations, 1905–1950*. New Brunswick, NJ: Rutgers University Press.

Li, M., & Bray, M. (2007). Cross-border flows of students for higher education: Push-pull factors and motivations of mainland Chinese students in Hong Kong and Macau. *Higher Education, 53*, 791–818.

Liu, Y. (2015, September 1). China's Nouveau Riche Have Landed on America's Campuses. *Foreign Policy*.

Mazzarol, T., Kemp, S., & Savery, L. (1997). *International students who choose not to study in Australia: An examination of Taiwan and Indonesia*. Canberra: Policy, Research and Analysis Section, Australian International Education Foundation.

Mazzarol, T., & Soutar, G. N. (2002). "Push-pull" factors influencing international student destination choice. *International Journal of Educational Management, 16*(2), 82–90.

McMahon, M. E. (1992). Higher education in a world market: A historical look at the global context of international study. *Higher Education, 24*(4), 465–482.

Ministry of Education. (2015, July 30). The 2014 education *communiqué*. Retrieved from the Ministry of Education website: http://www.moe.edu.cn/srcsite/A03/s180/moe_633/201508/t20150811_199589.html

Ministry of Education. (2016). *Blue book on returned overseas Chinese graduates and employment 2015*.

Ministry of Education. (2019). Statistics on Chinese citizens who went abroad in 2018. Retrieved October 15, 2019, from http://www.moe.gov.cn/jyb_xwfb/gzdt_gzdt/s5987/201903/t20190327_375704.html

New Oriental. (2015). *White book of China's study abroad*. Beijing: New Oriental Vision Overseas.

OECD. (2014). *Education at a glance*. Paris: Organization for Economic Co-operation and Development.

OECD. (2019). *Education at a glance*. Paris: Organization for Economic Co-operation and Development.

Oxford Economics. (2013). *The costs and benefits of international students: A report for the University of Sheffield*. Retrieved from the University of Sheffield website: https://www.sheffield.ac.uk/polopoly_fs/1.259052!/file/sheffield-international-students-report.pdf

Perkins, R., & Neumayer, E. (2014). Geographies of educational mobilities: Exploring the uneven flows of international students. *The Geographical Journal, 180*(3), 246–259.

Popadiuk, N. E. (2009). Unaccompanied Asian secondary students studying in Canada. *International Journal of Advanced Counselling, 31*, 229–243.

Ravenstein, E. G. (1885). The laws of migration. *Journal of the Royal Statistical Society, 48*(2), 167–227.

Rogers, K. (1984). Foreign students: Economic benefit or liability: Practical advice for colleges or universities that want to attract foreign students. *The College Board Review, 133*, 20–25.

Shih, K. Y. (2016). Transnational families. In C. L. Shehan (Ed.), *The Wiley Blackwell encyclopedia of family studies* (pp. 1–7). Indianapolis, IN: John Wiley & Sons.

Sina Education. (2015). *Number of test takers and admission rate for College-Entrance Examination, 1977–2014*. Retrieved from http://edu.sina.com.cn/gaokao/2015-06-18/1435473862.shtml

Stiglitz, J. E. (2006). *Making globalization work*. New York, NY: W. W. Norton & Company.

Stouffer, S. A. (1940). Intervening opportunities and competing migration. *Journal of Regional Science, 2*, 1–26.

Tan, J. (2013). Introduction. *The international mobility of students in Asia and the Pacific*. Retrieved from the UNESCO website: http://unesdoc.unesco.org/images/0022/002262/226219E.pdf

The Economist. (2010, August 5). *Foreign university students: Will they still come*. Retrieved September 29, 2015, from http://www.economist.com/node/16743639

Throsby, C. D. (1991). The financial impact of foreign student enrolments. *Higher Education, 21*(3), 351–358.

Throsby, C. D. (1999). *Financing and effects of internationalization in higher education: The economic costs and benefits of international student flows*. Retrieved from the Organisation for Economic Co-operation and Development website: https://www.oecd.org/sti/inno/2093396.pdf

To, W. M., Lung, J. W. Y., Lai, L. S. L., & Lai, T. M. (2014). Destination choice of cross-border Chinese students: An importance-performance analysis. *Educational Studies, 40*(1), 63–80.

Tsong, Y., & Liu, Y. (2009). Parachute kids and astronaut families. In N. Tewari & A. N. Alvarez (Eds.), *Asian American psychology: Current perspectives* (pp. 365–379). New York, NY: Psychology Press.

U.S. Immigration and Customs Enforcement (2014, November 2). Former Bay Area university president sentenced to more than 16 years in prison for visa fraud scheme. Accessed from https://www.ice.gov/news/releases/former-bay-area-university-president-sentenced-more-16-years-prison-visa-fraud-scheme

UNESCO. (2009). *Global Education Digest 2009: Comparing education statistics across the world*. Retrieved from the UNESCO website: http://unesdoc.unesco.org/images/0018/001832/183249e.pdf

Wallerstein, I. (2004). *World-system analysis: An introduction*. Durham, NC: Duke University Press.

Wu, X., & Lu, Y. (2002). The pressure faced by higher education institutions against their expansion and some policy discussion. *Guangxi Higher Education Research, 1*, 39–41.

Yue, C. (2013). International student mobility: China. *The international mobility of students in Asia and the Pacific*. Retrieved from the UNESCO website: http://unesdoc.unesco.org/images/0022/002262/226219E.pdf

Zhou, M. (1998). "Parachute kids" in southern California: The educational experience of Chinese children in transnational families. *Educational Policy, 12*, 682–704.

Chapter 2
Making Waves: A Historical Perspective on Overseas Chinese Students and China's Quest for Modernization

Introduction

While the concept of a foreign or international student may seem like a fairly recently emerged phenomenon, closely related as it is to the modern concept of the nation-state, the notion of leaving one's community and travelling or sojourning for educational purposes has in fact long existed in human history. As Du Bois (1956) states: "The pursuit of learning beyond the boundaries of one's own community, nation, or culture is as old as learning itself" (p. 1). The reason is that "[w]e need a constant cross-fertilization of ideas between the many cultures of mankind" (Caldwell, 1965, p. 69). Ancient Greeks, for example, were among the first to attract and host foreign students who came from faraway regions (Bevis & Lucas, 2007; Walden, 1909).

As early as the Sui Dynasty (581–618), China played host to foreign students, and during the Tang Dynasty (618–907) foreign students began arriving in China in relatively large numbers. For example, Japan sent delegations to China 13 times during the Tang Dynasty. It was estimated that the total number of Japanese students and monks who came with the delegations to learn about Confucianism, Buddhism, and other aspects of Chinese culture and Chinese history, amounted to 150 (Dong, 2003). If it was the prosperity and openness of a strong China that attracted students and scholars from Japan, Korea, Vietnam, and Russia in ancient China, it was the loss of its dominant position to the Western world after a series of defeats in wars and the ensuing unbalanced treaties that prompted China to gradually adopt the policy of sending Chinese students to study overseas.

On December 26, 1978, the first dispatch of 50 Chinese scholars and scientists, funded by the Chinese government, left for the United States. This would mark the beginning of a new wave of Chinese students studying overseas after decades of national isolation. Over the course of the subsequent four decades, that wave would grow ever stronger, and by the end of 2015, the total number of Chinese students

© Springer Nature Singapore Pte Ltd. 2020
B. Cheng et al., *The New Journey to the West*, Education in the Asia-Pacific
Region: Issues, Concerns and Prospects 53,
https://doi.org/10.1007/978-981-15-5588-6_2

studying overseas had reached 4.04 million with an average yearly increasing rate of 19.06%. In 2018, there were 662,100 Chinese students studying abroad, an increase of 8.83% over the previous year (Ministry of Education, 2019).

This new wave of Chinese students studying overseas can be seen as the continuation of the Chinese people's quest for self-strengthening through learning from the West. From *Yung Wing*, the father of the movement to send Chinese students overseas for study, to the first wave of China's 120 "fortunate sons" who studied in the United States between 1872 and 1881, to the second wave of Chinese students which included those going to Japan after 1895 and those studying in the United States on the Boxer Indemnity Scholarship between 1909 and 1940, and finally to this new, third wave of the present day, there is a common theme that runs throughout this nearly 200 years of history: How can China become a modern nation capable of competing with the West on the international scene?

This chapter is the first attempt to depict a thorough picture of those historical trends which bear significant connections with and thus important implications for the current wave. Through providing detailed and comprehensive information on those two waves of historical trends, this chapter shows that educational exchange has always been considered and used by the Chinese government as the most effective way for China to catch up with the more developed and industrialized countries, in spite of opposing voices from more conservative officials. Further, due to the high hopes placed on those exchange programs and the changes resulting from those programs, officials who initiated the programs and students who participated, in spite of their great contributions to and impact on the modernization of China, are susceptible to criticisms and distrust, and the perceptions of them have pendulated between patriots and traitors, heroes and villains, and vanguard and scapegoat (Bieler, 2004; Wang, 2013). That may be a common dilemma faced by anyone trying to build a bridge between two worlds.

Yung Wing, the Forerunner of Overseas Chinese Students

Yung Wing (a.k.a. *Rong Hong*, or *Jung Hung*), the first Chinese person ever to be awarded a degree from an American university, is considered a forerunner of overseas Chinese students. As LaFargue (1987) comments:

> He was the first Chinese in modern times to break completely away from the age-old Chinese social environment and to divorce himself from the cultural inheritance of his people. He marks an important point in the history of his country, for from him there stems in an ever widening stream that numerous body of young Chinese who, first in the mission schools in China and later in the colleges and universities of Europe and the United States, have become thoroughly imbued with the 'western viewpoint' and who have consciously striven to spread this viewpoint among their own people. ·

Yung Wing was born in 1828, the third child of four, in the village of *Nanping*, some four miles away from the then Portuguese-controlled trading colony of Macao. *Yung's* parents viewed Western schooling—where he could learn English—as a potential avenue for a career in business and diplomacy, and thus at the age of 7, he was sent to study for a 4-year period at a missionary school in Macao which was established in 1835 by Mrs. Gutzlaff, the wife of the British missionary, the Reverend Charles Gutzlaff. When the missionary school was closed, Yung returned to his village and stayed there for 2 years. Between 1841 and 1846, he attended the Morison School, first in Macao, and later in Hong Kong, where the school was moved in 1842. The Morison School was run by the Reverend. S. R. Brown, an 1832 graduate of Yale, and his wife. Toward the end of 1846, the Reverend Brown had decided to return to America, offering to take a few pupils with him to finish their education there. *Yung Wing* quite literally jumped at this opportunity. As he himself describes: "When he [the Reverend Brown] requested those who wished to accompany him to the States to signify it by rising, I was the first one on my feet" (Yung, 1909, p. 6). Through the influence of the Reverend Brown, *Yung Wing* and two other boys, *Wong Shing* and *Wong Foon*, were able to receive financial support from several patrons in Hong Kong who were not only to cover their education, but also support their parents during their absence in America.

In April 1847, the three boys, along with the Reverend Brown, arrived in New York after 98 days of voyaging on the ship "Huntress." Soon after in that same year, the three boys started attending the Monson Academy in Massachusetts. Gradually their life took different courses: In 1848, *Wong Shing* returned to China due to poor health; *Wong Foon*, upon graduating from the Monson Academy in 1850, entered the University of Edinburgh; and *Yung Wing* started his college education at Yale at the age of 22.

The first year in college proved to be difficult for *Yung Wing* largely because of his underpreparedness, especially in such subjects as Latin, Greek, and mathematics. As he describes: "I used to sweat over my studies until twelve o'clock every night the whole Freshman year" (Yung, 1909, p. 6). He worked so hard to keep up with his studies, while also making ends meet financially, that his health suffered. Although he himself felt that he did not perform well academically throughout his college course, so much so that he actually thought he might be dismissed, he was actually quite well-known on campus for his strong academic performance. As the first Chinese to receive an education at a first-class American college, he naturally attracted considerable attention, and he proved himself to be worthy of the attention by winning the first prize in English composition for the two consecutive years of sophomore and junior, and by actively participating in such extracurricular activities as debating. LaFargue (1987) thus comments on him: "*Yung Wing's* career at Yale was successful. He was well-known and very much liked among his classmates. He seems to have had a facility for absorbing his American environment" (p. 22).

Behind the stamina and perseverance which supported him through the difficult yet rewarding college years was his deep love for China and a strong sense of social responsibility toward the Chinese people. Between his own financial struggle and academic exertion, he never forgot "the lamentable condition of China." As he put it: For the 8 years of sojourn in America, China "had never escaped my mind's eye nor my heart's yearning for her welfare." He reached the following conclusion: "the rising generation of China should enjoy the same educational advantage that I had enjoyed; that through western education China may be regenerated, become enlightened and powerful" (Yung, 1909, pp. 15–16). Having thought much about the future of China and his possible role in better preparing China for the modern world, he became convinced that "China's only hope was to … adopt as rapidly as possible the technological, progressive civilization of the Occident." It seemed to him that the best way to do it was for the Chinese government to send abroad "a constant stream of carefully selected Chinese youths to be educated at the schools of America and Europe" (LaFargue, 1987, p. 23). It was toward this goal of enabling more Chinese to enjoy a Western education that *Yung Wing* directed his efforts and energy from 1854 to 1872.

Upon graduating from Yale in 1854, he embarked on his journey back to China. After 6 months of readjustment in Canton, including recovering written and spoken Chinese, he began experimenting with different careers to make a living while awaiting the right opportunity to implement his ideas of reform. *Yung* first worked briefly as the secretary of Dr. Peter Parker, the US Commissioner in Canton, then followed this with an unsuccessful attempt to become an attorney in Hong Kong. Subsequently, having served at the Imperial Customs Translating Department in Shanghai, *Yung* would finally come to gradually establish himself as a successful businessman by trading tea and silk.

The First Wave: The Chinese Educational Mission (1872–1881)

The first wave of Chinese students going overseas to study consisted of a few government-sponsored overseas educational missions in the 1870s and 1880s. For example, between 1877 and 1897, the government sent 85 cadets from the Fuzhou Shipyard School to England and France to study engineering and technology. *Yan Fu*, who later became a renowned translator and important pioneer in the effort to introduce Western writings on social science to Chinese readers, was among the first Chinese students to study at the Royal Naval College Greenwich in England (Chen, 1997; Lin, 2016).

The best known among the first group of overseas Chinese students were the 120 youth who studied in America between 1872 and 1881. Due to his unremitting efforts from 1854 and 1871, *Yung Wing* gradually won support from enlightened high-ranking officials such as *Zeng Guofan* and *Li Hongzhang*. In a memorial presented in 1871 to the emperor by these two figures, who were arguably the most influential officials of the time, *Zeng* and *Li* made a strong case for acquiring technical knowledge of the West if China ever hoped to be free from foreign aggression. Further, they argued that sending students to study overseas was the quickest and most effective way to acquire Western technology. The imperial court finally approved the plan for sending groups of students to the United States, which was called the "Chinese Educational Mission" (CEM hereafter). The plan was to send 30 Chinese students aged between 12 and 16 each year for four consecutive years between 1872 and 1875. These 120 students would study in America for 15 years, and upon graduating from American colleges, would return to China in 1887 to serve the country (Bieler, 2004; LaFargue, 1987; Wang, 2013). In the summer of 1872, the first 30 students sailed for the United States, and they were followed by three more groups of 30 students each year for the following three consecutive years. These 120 students were called "China's first hundred" (LaFargue, 1987) and referred to as the "fortunate sons" (Leibovitz & Miller, 2011).

Chinese Context and Motives

While *Yung Wing* was biding his time preparing to implement the plan to send young Chinese overseas to study, China itself was undergoing important changes. The mid-nineteenth century was a turning point in Chinese history in terms of both the internal decline of the Qing dynasty due to such factors as territorial expansion and continual warfare, an explosive increase in population, and bureaucratic corruption, as well as social upheavals like the Taiping Rebellion (1850–1864), and the increasing external pressure from the impending menace of foreign invasions with the Anglo-French military presence in Beijing (Chen, 1997; Luo, 1997). The loss of the Opium War to the British in 1842, which, among other things, forced China to open five southern ports to western traders, was a wake-up call for some officials in the Qing court, who became reluctantly open to the knowledge and power of Western countries, and for Chinese intellectuals who then started seeking and disseminating Western learning in hopes of "learning technology from the barbarians to contain them," as advocated by *Lin Zexu* and *Wei Yuan* (Bieler, 2004, p. 3). Gradually, China ended its isolationist policy, which had been implemented from the late seventeenth century, and grew increasingly open to the influence of Western culture (Chen, 1997; Lin, 2016).

One of the approaches to strengthen China, which was discussed at the Qing court in the 1860s, was to introduce Western technology, and in 1863 the possibility of sending students abroad began to be debated. It was within this historical context that the implementation of *Yung Wing*'s reform ideas were made possible.

American Context and Motives

America's motives for drawing international students to its educational institutions are in part political, sociocultural, academic, and economic. Academic motives are often cited as the main reason for encouraging foreign students to come to America to study, but even a cursory examination of American policies indicates that from the very beginning, political and sociocultural motives were the driving forces. It is only in recent years that economic considerations have become increasingly important motives.

In the early years of American history, the idea of educational exchange was not welcomed by either the public or politicians. One reason is that sending students to study in European universities amounted to acknowledging that American higher education was inferior. Further, many Americans did not favor reinforcing the ties to Europe through educational exchanges. Thomas Jefferson, for example, was an adamant opponent of sending students to study in any European country, including Germany. He maintained that "an American, coming to Europe for education, loses in his knowledge, in his morals, in his health, and in his habits." Washington had an even more nationalistic view of educational exchange believing that "there was a danger in sending American youth abroad among other political systems when they had not well learned the value of their own" (Bevis & Lucas, 2007, pp. 32–33).

Following the same line of logic, it is no surprise that America would regard educational exchange as "an instrument of foreign policy and of national interest" when the world started to come to America for higher education (Du Bois, 1956, p. 12). It is argued that "American political and educational leaders hoped that on returning home, the graduates of these academic programs would act as ambassadors and spread American political and cultural mores in their respective nations—to cultivate sympathy and understanding for American values worldwide" (Bevis & Lucas, 2007, p. 245).

Arrangement and Life in America

America was chosen as the destination for the CEM, instead of Great Britain, France or Germany, partially because *Yung Wing* was familiar with the American educational system, and partially because of the Burlingame Treaty which had been signed between the United States and China in 1868. The treaty was named after Anson Burlingame, the first American minister to reside in Beijing (1861–1867). This treaty allowed citizens of the two countries to have mutual rights of residence and attendance at public schools (LaFargue, 1987). Another reason for favoring America as the destination country was that Chinese officials seemed to believe that an American education was more practical than a European one (Bieler, 2004).

The recruitment was not easy partially because the rather generous offer from the government to educate the students and pay their families a modest stipend while they were abroad, met with some suspicion among the local Chinese population. Families were also reluctant to see their children disappear to an unknown land for such a long period of time. For the first detachment of 30 boys, *Yung Wing* had to go on recruitment tours throughout the Canton area to persuade families (Bevis & Lucas, 2007). Out of the 120 boys who were finally recruited, 70% of them were from the region around Canton where the local people had more exposure to foreigners and foreign influence (LaFargue, 1987; Yung, 1909).

The average age of the students in the CEM was 12 and a half, and they were placed in groups of two and three with American families (Bevis & Lucas, 2007; LaFargue, 1987). They were required to wear long Chinese gowns and plaited cues, but they were ridiculed by their American classmates, as to the American sensibility of the time, they looked like girls. As teenagers who were sensitive to how they were perceived, the students were determined to abandon the long gown for American trousers and coats. In the few cases where they cut their cues, they were immediately sent back to China. Overall they seemed to be adjusting well in the strange land. As LaFargue (1987) describes:

> They became Americanized with bewildering rapidity. In no time they learned the language of the schoolroom and the playground. They soon shed their long silk gowns and with them their dignified Chinese manners. Within a few months they were on the best of terms with their American schoolmates and were competing for honors both in their classes and on the baseball diamond. In their American homes they were taught western table manners and were introduced to the somewhat severe discipline of New England family life (p. 35).

Termination of the Mission

The changes the boys underwent, which were inevitable to some extent, were viewed negatively by the Chinese officials who co-directed the Mission with *Yung Wing*, and a stream of unfavorable reports were sent back to Peking on the "un-Chinese conduct of the students" (LaFargue, 1987, p. 44). With the death of *Zeng Guofan* in 1871, the most important supporter of the Mission, the Conservatives gradually came back to power at the court. They saw abolishing the Mission as a way to attack *Li Hongzhang*, the protégé of *Zeng*. Further, the high cost of running the Mission—an estimated total of one million two-hundred thousand taels[1] and an average of $1200 per student per year—had truly been a tremendous amount for China and thus a source of concern and conflict as China was struggling financially (Bieler, 2004; LaFargue, 1987).

During this same period, an anti-Chinese mentality had begun to take shape in America. The "gold rush," which started in 1847 in California, brought thousands of Chinese to America who were forced to stay and find work as most of them failed

---

[1] A former Chinese monetary unit based on the value of a tael of standard silver, which was a measure of weight used in China and East Asia, of varying amount but fixed in China at 50 g (1 3/4 oz.).

to make their fortune. Many of them were able to find employment in the construction of the first transcontinental railroad in America, a significant and widely recognized contribution to the growth of the country. After the completion of the railroad, however, the Chinese were back in the labor market, which had grown more competitive due to the recession following the Civil War, and the large influx of settlers from the eastern part of the country into the west. Resentment of the Chinese workers, who were considered the "yellow peril," grew among American workers, and "Chinese workers became targets of racial attacks and mob violence" (Bevis & Lucas, 2007, p. 56; Bieler, 2004, p. 7). As a response to the mounting anti-Chinese sentiment and social unrest, in May 1882, the American congress passed the *Chinese Exclusion Act* prohibiting Chinese laborers from entering the United States (Bevis & Lucas, 2007; Ye, 2001). In the midst of anti-Chinese sentiments, the American government rescinded its earlier agreement with the Chinese government to allow Chinese students to study at military academies in the United States. This was a huge disappointment for *Li Hongzhang* as in his mind military training was the main motive for the CEM (Bieler, 2004; LaFargue, 1987). As Ye argues: "The anti-Chinese zealotry of the American policy makers as well as the American government's refusal to admit Chinese students into U.S. military academies had given the conservative Chinese officials a convincing excuse to call back the educational mission" (Ye, 2001, p. 88).

In 1881, *Yung Wing* received the final orders to abandon the Mission, and all teachers and students were to return to China. By the time the students returned to China in 1881, only two had completed college at the Sheffield Scientific School of Yale University. Even though over 60 of them were enrolled in colleges and technical schools, most of them had only started their training (Bevis & Lucas, 2007; LaFargue, 1987).

On the surface, the Mission was terminated for political and economic reasons, as discussed in the preceding analysis. At a deeper level, however, the failure of the Mission was almost doomed from its inception for ideological reasons. The conservatives at the court were opposed to the Mission from the very beginning because they felt the plan of sending students abroad seriously undermined Chinese tradition and Confucian values (Bieler, 2004). This expression of what is referred to as the *ti-yong* dichotomy would present a dilemma for the Chinese journey to modernization.

Along with the intellectual enlightenment came the *Yangwu* Movement, which is essentially a "self-strengthening movement" (Bieler, 2004, p. 4) that aimed to introduce Western technology into China. Led by high-ranking officials such as *Zeng Guofan, Li Hongzhang,* and *Zhang Zhidong*, the Movement was governed by the principle of *Zhongti Xiyong* (Chinese learning as the essential principles and Western learning as the practical application). The *ti-yong* dichotomy can be traced back to the mid-nineteenth century. *Ti,* (essential principles), is composed of two elements: one is the feudal, totalitarian political system, and the other is Confucian ethics. *Yong* (practical applications) refers to Western science and technology. *Ti* is the goal and *yong* the method which serves *ti* (Chen, 1997; Wang, 1997). According to Chen (1997), there is a contradiction inherent in the principle of *Zhongti Xiyong*, between the feudalist goals and the capitalist means: adherence to the essential principles of Chinese learning confined the *Yangwu* Movement to only a superficial knowledge of the West, "for the steady dissemination of Western learning without limitations would have eventually broken down the feudalist *ti*" (p. 166).

This ideological dilemma of *ti-yong* was reflected in the conflicts between *Yung Wing* and the other conservative co-directors. Along with *Yung Wing*, another Chinese official, *Qin Lanpin*, who was known for his devotion to Confucian learning, was appointed to co-direct the mission. When *Qin* was called back to China in 1878, the even more conservative *Wu Zideng* replaced him. The trigger of the termination was the neglect of Chinese studies on the boys' part as they were supposed to be instructed in the Chinese language and Confucian classics by Chinese teachers who accompanied the Mission during school breaks (Bieler, 2004; LaFargue, 1987). Both *Qin* and *Wu* were astonished and upset to see the boys had been "denationalized" (Bieler, 2004, p. 7) and "Americanized" (Bevis & Lucas, 2007, p. 49). For example, *Wu* scolded the students for not kneeling down to him, a sign of respect for elders. Many of them preferred Western suits over their Chinese gowns, and some had cut their queues. Further, it was disturbing to the conservative officials that some students had become Christians (Bevis & Lucas, 2007; Bieler, 2004).

Yung Wing, on the other hand, was convinced that "China's future depended on these students abandoning their traditions, fully taking on the science and technology of Western culture, as soon as possible" (Bevis & Lucas, 2007, p. 73). His emphasis on American studies at the expense of Chinese studies came as no surprise, and his encouragement of the boys to break with the Chinese tradition and habits essentially "betrayed the Chinese government's original purpose of assimilating and using Western technology while preserving traditional culture" (Bevis & Lucas, 2007, p. 73). He did not seem "to have been disturbed by the evident fact that in the measure that China adopted the machinery of the West, the old traditional Chinese civilization would be undermined and eventually destroyed" (LaFargue, 1987, p. 28). This approach of wholesale Westernization has important implications and sowed the seeds for the criticism of blind copying on the part of Chinese students returning home, and also partially explained the premature termination of the CEM (Bevis & Lucas, 2007). As LaFargue (1987) summarizes: "His attitude opened the conduct of the Mission to severe criticism by those in China unfavorably disposed towards it, and in the long run it was one of the chief reasons why the Mission was prematurely abandoned" (p. 35).

The CEM started around the same time that Japan's diplomatic Iwakura Mission (1871–1873) took place, but their different destiny in some way forecasted the fate of the two nations in their modernization process. While the Iwakura Mission expedited the Meiji Restoration and helped Japan develop national policy for the realization of modernization (Ding, 1997; Wang, 1997), the CEM was ended 9 years later in 1881—much earlier than the originally planned 15 years—when only 2 out of the 120 students were able to complete their college education. To a certain extent, it is this underlying ideological dilemma of *ti-yong* that terminated the CEM and shattered *Yung Wing*'s dream of strengthening China by sending students to study overseas.

Contributions by Yung Wing and the 120 "Fortunate Sons"

Yung Wing died in 1912 in Hartford, Connecticut, having spent almost half of his lifetime in the United States. He was highly regarded by the next generation of students in America as an "Educator, Reformer, Statesman, Patriot" (Bieler, 2004, p. 16). He was often criticized, however, for his lack of Chineseness and disrespect for the Chinese culture and was considered by many "a comprador whose thoughts reflected signs of cultural imperialism" (Wang, 2013, p. 32). It is true that *Yung Wing* was converted to Christianity while studying at Monson Academy in Massachusetts (1847–1849), and in 1852 he became a naturalized American citizen (which was later revoked under *the Naturalization Act* of 1870). He even married an American woman, Mary L. Kellogg, the daughter of a prominent local doctor in Hartford, in 1875 (Bieler, 2004; LaFargue, 1987). As Edmund Worthy argues, "His loyalty to America rested on his family ties as well as on a strong intellectual kinship with the West" (Wang, 2013, p. 33). Nonetheless, his affinities with America did not prevent him from loving China. He describes this seeming paradox the following way: "Would it not be strange, if an Occidental education, continually exemplified by an Occidental civilization, had not wrought upon an Oriental such a metamorphosis in his inward nature as to make him feel and act as though he were a being coming from a different world, when he confronted one so diametrically different. This was precisely my case, and yet neither my patriotism nor love of my fellow-countrymen had been weakened" (Yung, 1909, *Preface*).

Yung's contribution to the modernization process of China should not be underestimated. As LaFargue argues: "[*Yung Wing*]… more than any other one person, prepared the ground for China's advances in science and technology. His protégés, the students of the Educational Mission, were the active leaders in establishing modern communications in China" (LaFargue, 1987, p. 65). Together they built railroads, constructed telegraph lines, developed coal mines, became China's first modern army and navy officers, and filled the ranks of her consular and diplomatic service. According to LaFargue, among the 100 or so members of the CEM who did return to China to serve, 13 worked in the diplomatic service; 6 in coal mining; 14 worked as either chief engineers or in managerial capacities in railroads; 17 served in the navy, 7 of whom were killed in action and 2 of whom became admirals; 15 contributed to the Government Telegraph Administration; 4 practiced medicine; 3 worked in education; 2 served in the Customs Service; and 12 became magistrates and governors, etc., following the traditional career routine (LaFargue, 1987).

Although the CEM members "never rose far up the ladder of official preferment" (LaFargue, 1987, p. 65) as a group, there are names that bear significant positions in modern Chinese history. Among them are *Zhan Tianyou*, the first engineer to have constructed an important railway—the Peking-Zhangjiakou railway—independent of foreign assistance; *Tang Shaoyi*, the first Prime Minister and one of the founders of the Chinese Republic which was established after the 1911 revolution; *Liang Dun*yan, who served as the Minister of Communications in the first Republican government, and the minister of foreign affairs; and *Cai Tingkai*, who rose to the position of a navy admiral (Bevis & Lucas, 2007; Bieler, 2004; LaFargue, 1987).

Sun Yat-Sen in Hawaii

Although not as part of the CEM, *Sun Yat-Sen*, the founding father of the Republic of China, came to the United States around the same period of time and he seemed to have shared some common experiences as those 120 boys as an international sojourner. All his lifetime *Sun* paid six visits to Hawaii between 1879 and 1910, among which only the first one was for educational purpose. He first came to Hawaii in 1879 at the age of 13 with the help of his older brother *Sun Mei* who had come in 1871 and become an economic success. He enrolled in Iolani School between 1879 and 1882, where he quickly mastered English, from not knowing a word of the language. He graduated from Iolani School as the second in grammar and was awarded a prize by King Kalakaua. He then continued his education at the Punahou School (then called Oahu College), but was there only for one semester in the spring of 1883. He was sent back to China by his brother who felt that he had started to betray Chinese culture when *Sun* expressed his wish to become a Christian (Lum & Lum, 1999).

Needless to say, the early years *Sun* spent in Hawaii for his education were the most formative period of his time there and had significant implications for his later, revolutionary career. As Lum and Lum (1999) state: "During his years at Iolani and Punahou, he was exposed to Western culture, was strongly influenced by it, and in his young mind, the seeds of Western democracy were planted." Even *Sun* himself told a journalist in 1910: "This is my Hawaii ... here I was brought up and educated; and it was here that I came to know what modern civilized governments are like and what they mean" (p. 3).

The Second Wave (1890s–1940s)

While China was debating about the merit of *ti* and *yong*, the Western world became more industrialized, and significant changes took place by the late nineteenth century: More telegraph lines and steamships were built, cities grew, more goods were traded, and bank offices appeared. If the defeat in the Opium War (1840–1842) was a wake-up call for China, Social Darwinism, with its credos of the struggle for existence, natural selection, and survival of the fittest, offered an explanation of the rules of the game. Japan's crushing victory over China in the 1895 Sino-Japanese War prompted the Chinese government to take immediate measures to obtain Western knowledge and technology, including reforming its educational system and sending students overseas to study. As Harrell states: "[There was] a new openness, a new focus on national goals, a general acceptance of the need to modernize, a hint that reform outside tradition was worth considering" (Harrell, 1992, p. 5; Wang, 2013).

It is under this historical and social context that Chinese students began to go in large numbers to Europe, Japan, and America, thus forming the second wave of Chinese students studying overseas. The lingering question was once again pushed to the forefront: How can China become a modern nation capable of competing with the West? Again, sending students overseas was endorsed as the quickest and most effective way to reform education and modernize China. Similar to the first wave, the main goal of the second wave was also to strengthen the state by modernizing its economy, military, and education. The gradual phasing out of the civil service examination system and its final abolition in 1905 removed institutional barriers and provided an additional catalyst to the trend of Chinese students studying overseas; the route to upward social mobility was now clearly found in obtaining an education in foreign countries (Harrell, 1992).

Important components of this second wave include students studying in Japan after the 1895 Sino-Japanese War and students studying in America on the Boxer Indemnity Scholarship after 1909. The following sections will examine those two groups.

The 1895 Sino-Japanese War and Chinese Students in Japan

After the defeat of China in the 1895 Sino-Japanese War, Japan became an increasingly popular destination for overseas Chinese students. First, its language, literature, and customs were similar to those of China, and this cultural affinity meant that students would be less likely to become "denationalized" (Bieler, 2004, p. 7). Further, its physical proximity meant lower transportation and living cost, which made it a more financially affordable proposition (Bieler, 2004; Harrell, 1992).

Another reason for Chinese students' interest in studying in Japan, which is arguably the most important one, was Japan's success in its modernization efforts. Japan, an Asian nation, had built its national power to qualify as a competitor with the West which drew admiration from Asian countries, including China. As Ye states: "To many [Chinese] people in the first decade of the 1900s, recently modernized Japan was a shortcut to Western knowledge" (Ye, 2001, p. 9) This "[l]earning about the West through Japan" (Harrell, 1992, p. 7) had become the primary driving force behind the large number of Chinese students going to Japan.

From the Japanese perspective, having Chinese students study within its borders fit well with its vision of "Asia for the Asians" and "common culture." These students, many of whom might become part of China's next generation of leaders, could help to expand Japanese influence throughout Asia. In other words, both sides welcomed the prospect of educational exchange which was viewed mutually beneficial as it ultimately "[held] promise of developing a counterforce against the bogey that faced them both—the threatening presence of the West in East Asia" (Harrell, 1992, p. 7).

In 1896, 13 young Chinese arrived in Tokyo—the first to study in Japan. The number quickly and steadily increased in the following years and in the peak year of 1905–1906, about 8000–9000 Chinese were studying in Tokyo alone. However, the number began to decrease in 1906, mainly because of the competition from the opportunity to study in America (Wang, 2013). It was estimated that between 1900 and 1911, as many as 20,000 Chinese students received education in Japan. Unlike students in the first wave, a considerable proportion of Chinese students who studied in Japan came from privileged family backgrounds, and many of them were self-funded. The majority of them pursued liberal arts, teacher training, and military studies, and only a small number studied science and technology majors (Harrell, 1992).

Even though it is true that Japanese and Chinese cultures share similarities, adjusting to life in Japan still proved to be difficult for most Chinese students. In fact, among the first 13 students who studied in Japan starting in 1896, only seven eventually completed their education and received diplomas. Homesickness was a common problem among them, partially because of the differences in food, dress, and customs which made them an "object of curiosity" and the "butt of jokes" (Harrell, 1992, p. 2). Furthermore, the overall quality of education they received was poor because Japan was not well equipped to accommodate so many Chinese students (Bieler, 2004). The most challenging difficulty for those students, however, was the arrogant and patronizing attitude of Japanese toward Chinese, which resulted in an environment of indifference and even hostility. For centuries the Chinese culture had been respected and emulated by the Japanese, but now China was perceived as "antediluvian in a modern world of technological advance" (Harrell, 1992, p. 81). Deeply aware of the depiction of China as the objects of derision in Japanese press, Chinese students often felt inferior and alienated which easily slipped into the feelings of resentment and hostility toward Japan (Bieler, 2004; Harrell, 1992). The maladjustment of those Chinese students was to a large extent due to the fact that it was not in the interest of either side to help those students fit into the new environment by developing intercultural understanding. In fact, "it was thought better that Chinese not intermingle with Japanese" (Harrell, 1992, p. 8). The objective of China was to learn about the West through Japan, not to learn about Japan, and what the Japanese side stressed was supervising the students for educational purposes.

Partially prompted by the contempt and alienation keenly felt by the Chinese students in Japan, many of them turned to such activities as forming organizations where they gained the experiences of public speaking and political debate. This can also explain why there were a large proportion of Chinese students studying in Japan who eventually became avowed revolutionaries and made significant contribution to the 1911 Revolution which overthrew the Qing imperial rule. In their quest for an independent and powerful China, many students started to re-examine the traditional Chinese culture, and they identified aspects of deficiencies in China's national character which they thought worked to the advantage of intruding foreigners. For example, most of them agreed that Chinese people had a passive and servile tendency and this characteristic of subservice was "a disease permeating every aspect of Chinese life" (Harrell, 1992, p. 195). A related character deficiency they thought made China fall prey to foreign invasion and suppression was the lack of the concept of "public spirit" which meant that Chinese tended to put self-interest above the welfare of the community. Those students, equipped with a modern education and nationalist fervor, greatly accelerated the pace of change in China as a new social force. As Harrell (1992) argues:

> For them, exposure to the outside world created the desire to participate in China's political life, to help chart out a course for China's future. For them Asia for the Asians came to mean China for the Chinese, national independence and the strength to ward off all imperialists of whatever origin (p. 209).

The Boxer Indemnity Scholarship and Studying in America (1909–1940s)

After the invasion of China by the eight allied forces of Britain, France, the United States, Germany, Russia, Japan, Italy, and Austria between 1900 and 1901, China was forced to pay 450 million taels (an equivalent of $330 million) to these eight countries as a compensation for their losses in the war. This payment is called the Boxer Indemnity. The United States received about 7.5%, or $25 million. After a long debate and much negotiation, the United States decided to return the surplus part of the Boxer Indemnity, under the stipulation that the money be spent on educating Chinese students in the United States (Bieler, 2004; Li, 2008).

From the American perspective, this educational plan would strengthen its ties with China so that the influence of a rising Japan in China could be contained to a certain extent. To the United States, Japan was a rival in Asia, and it had effectively grown its influence through both military victories and educational programs that allowed a large influx of Chinese students. Further, it would help to raise the prestige and image of the United States in China. Having successfully mentored Japan in its modernization process and deeply proud of this accomplishment, America hoped to do the same for China and have long-term influence on China's future. But, in contrast to the more strong arm technique employed by US Naval Commodore Matthew Perry with his ships off the shores of Japan nearly half a century earlier, as Bieler summarizes: "The educational plan was a more subtle and strategic policy than using gunboats to open China to American influence and commerce" (Bieler, 2004, p. 43; Ye, 2001).

Compared to the paradoxical ideological and intellectual environment which was dominated by the *ti-yong* dichotomy during the first wave, students in the early twentieth century were urged to acquire broad learning from the West (Bieler, 2004). As Ye states: "[It became] understood and largely accepted by the people involved that going abroad to study would imply a departure from traditional ways of life, in contrast to the resistance to Western cultural influences by the conservative officials in the *Yung Wing* mission" (Ye, 2001, p. 9). For China, the West represented both the humiliation of oppression and the lure of modernity. Further humiliated by the Boxer Incident—after losing both Opium Wars in 1842 and 1869, and the 1895 Sino-Japanese War, China became even more eager to strengthen itself through learning from the West. The Boxer Indemnity Program required that 80% of the students study technical and practical disciplines such as engineering, agriculture, and mining. China also hoped to build an alliance with America to counterbalance the increasing influence of neighboring Japan (Bieler, 2004; Ye, 2001).

Toward the end of 1908, President Roosevelt signed a bill remitting the indemnity. It was stipulated that the United States would return about $500,000 every year to China for establishing preparatory school and training 100 students a year to study in the United States, beginning in 1909, and the final payment would be made in 1940. In 1909 and 1925, the United States delivered the remission of the Boxer Indemnity in two installments (Bieler, 2004; Li, 2008). On October 12, 1909, the first group of Chinese students, a total of 47 winners from 640 candidates who had sat on a 5-day exam, sailed for the United States from Shanghai. The following year, 70 students passed the exam and left for the United States, and an additional 73 students in 1911. In 1911 the Imperial Tsinghua College was established with an enrollment of 468 students to help prepare students who were going to study in the United States. The college eventually became a comprehensive university in 1925, and the name was changed to Tsinghua University in 1927 (Li, 2008).

As "the most important scheme for educating Chinese students in America and arguably the most consequential and successful in the entire foreign-study movement of twentieth-century China" (Ye, 2001, p. 9), the Boxer Indemnity Scholarship Program contributed to the rapid and steady increase in the number of students in America. While there were only 300 of them in 1906, the number grew to 650 in 1911 and reached 1000 4 years later. By 1918, there were about 1200 Indemnity Scholarship recipients in America, and it was estimated that around 1600 Chinese students studied in America between 1925 and 1926. They tended to concentrate in schools located in the East and Midwest, and only a small number of them attended schools in the West and the South. They were also likely to have come from relatively privileged family backgrounds, similar to those who studied in Japan.

Yet another similarity to those Chinese students studying in Japan was that those who studied in America also had difficulties making adjustments. Needless to say, most of them were homesick. Inadequate English preparation, especially speaking, also added to the difficulty. What was the most challenging for them to deal with was the negative image of China and the racial discrimination they encountered. As described earlier, the early Chinese immigrants came to the United States as laborers, and the majority of them were poverty-stricken peasants. As a result, the image of the Chinese "coolie" had been formed and established roots among Americans from early on. During the first decades of the twentieth century, American popular culture portrayed the Chinese as "murderers, robbers, kidnappers, bloodthirsty priests, and even geisha keepers" (Bieler, 2004, p. 122) which "helped sustain and popularize the impression of mystery, peculiarity, backwardness, and dishonesty already associated with the Chinese" (Ye, 2001, p. 87). The passing of the *Chinese Exclusion Act* in 1882 also helped to perpetuate the anti-Chinese mentality, and it was not uncommon for Chinese students to encounter racial discrimination, such as open, verbal insults and refusals of service in restaurants. The following excerpt from the "American Conception of the Chinese" demonstrates the layers of misunderstanding of Chinese people among the American public (Bieler, 2004, p. 123):

> The average American: "They are Japs."
> The uneducated class: "Well, the Chinaman's chop suey is some class."
> The middle class: "Chinaman eats rats and birds' nests!" (Straw and twigs)
> The intelligent class: "The Chinese Revolution! Premier Kai and Dr. Sun!"

To make things even worse, when the students returned to China, they felt it difficult to find their niche in a changing society. The previously vibrant ambience of political reform of the late Qing Dynasty had disappeared, and the returnees—to their great disappointment—had become "disheartened spectators of warlord politics" (Ye, 2001, p. 43). For some, this meant the disillusionment of their ideals; for others, it meant the lack of employment opportunity. As Ye (2001) describes: "Many people have to give up what they've learned, and to take whatever job is available" (p. 66). Further, they were often criticized as "intolerant of opposition, unwilling to start at the bottom, disregarded details in their work, or lacked a steadfast purpose" (Bieler, 2004, p. 320). Even worse, they were often mistrusted and perceived to have been "Americanized," as reflected in the following image depicted in a short story of the time:

> He wore clothes of the best fashion, smoked, and used slang, and developed a keen interest in athletics; in short he was fast becoming Americanized. His ideas of life were changing too. Some of the old teachings which he had formerly regarded as infallible now appeared to him not only questionable but ridiculous. He began to lay more value on personal attraction and less on intellectual parts. He regarded riches as the highest prize of life and forgot his first resolution to dedicate his life to unselfish service (Bieler, 2004, p. 227).

Even though it is an insurmountable task to gauge the influence of the American-educated Chinese, it is no exaggeration to say that they played a part in the "cultural transformation of China" (Bieler, 2004, p. 227). The three specific spheres of their influence include education, government, and technology. Out of this generation of returned Chinese from America came major leaders in those areas, and it produced some of the most prominent professionals in diplomacy, industry, and finance, and important modern educators and scholars who exerted profound influence on the intellectual life during the first half of the twentieth century. Among the stellar group of modern Chinese intellectuals who emerged from this generation of American-educated returnees was *Hu Shi*, who later became the chief spokesperson for the May Fourth New Culture Movement during the 1910s and 1920s. Other influential figures include: *Yang Zhenning*, the 1957 Nobel Prize winner in physics; *Zhao Yuanren*, a pioneer in the fields of linguistics and musicology in China; *Zhu Kezhen*, a Harvard-trained meteorologist; and *Zhang Pengchun*, who made significant contributions to both education and theater in China. As Ye (2001) summarizes:

> The foundations these people laid in republican China, particularly in the areas of higher education, research, and, to a lesser degree, industry, eventually provided the institutional base of the People's Republic of China. ...they introduced new social customs, new kinds of interpersonal relationships, and new ways of associating in groups—in brief, they initiated a new way of life that contained key aspects of Chinese modernity (p. 2).

The Dilemma of Making Waves: Comparing and Contrasting

The two waves of Chinese students studying overseas took place in the historical context of China's humiliation by Western powers since 1840. Thus, the primary driving force behind the two waves was a patriotic mentality and a strong sense of social responsibility among the students to learn from the West so that China could end its humiliating history of being trampled upon, even though the need to catch up with the Western world seemed to be even more urgent during the second wave, and thus the approach was more wholesale.

For both waves, the high hopes for those students quickly turned into insurmountably high expectations. With such a heavy burden on their shoulders almost from the beginning, their failure to achieve these expectations comes as little surprise. As Bieler (2004) argues:

> [T]he Qing government expected too much from the first generation of students in the Chinese Educational Mission. The goal of making China technologically independent was unrealizable. The second generation of students was given an equally daunting set of goals in 1910: free China from foreign domination, abolish the practice of extraterritoriality, establish a parliamentary government, frame a constitution, and establish a new financial system and an effective military system (p. 342).

With such high expectations placed upon them, those students were of course susceptible to criticisms. One such criticism of returned students was the problem of "blind copying," referring to excessive reliance on foreign theories and methods which were often not applicable to China. Another criticism had to do with social stratification, in that "the concentration of Chinese students in Japan and the United States created a special political and social status for the returned scholars that further contributed to the 'Japanization' and 'Americanization' of Chinese society" (Bevis & Lucas, 2007, p. 73).

It was also those high expectations that caused the perceptions of those students to pendulate between patriots and traitors, heroes and villains, and vanguard and scapegoat (Bieler, 2004; Wang, 2013). On the one hand, the students were considered threats because of the Western values and knowledge they had been exposed to and oftentimes acquired. The cultural adjustments they had gone through made them the targets of suspicion because they could no longer be trusted as patriots. Their energy, independence, outspokenness, and ingenuity all seemed dangerous to the existing power structure in the eyes of Chinese officials. As a result, many of them returned to their places of study overseas, unable to call China home anymore because of the cold rebuff they received. They were paid low wages and kept low in ranks so that their influence could be lessened. On the other hand, their skills were needed in a China desperately seeking its way to modernization. LaFargue (1987) argues: "They not only saw the emergence of a 'new China'; they prepared the way" (p. 16). To a certain extent, it was the very success of the study-abroad programs and experiences that put those students in this dilemma. It is also a common dilemma faced by anyone who tries to build a bridge between two totally different worlds as they struggle to gain recognition or gratitude from either side.

Moving Forward with the Third Wave

In many aspects, the current third wave of Chinese students studying overseas differs from the two historical waves. For example, unlike the first two waves where China was forced to open its door by Western aggression and invasion, China made its choice to open up to the Western world toward the end of the 1970s, and thus educational exchange was more of a voluntary action. However, the goal was similar: Educational exchanges were used as a quick way to learn from the West so that China could keep up.

Further, the scale of transnational mobility for Chinese students is unprecedented, which is facilitated by the process of globalization. Globalization presents both opportunities and risks for international student mobility. On the one hand, mobility is made easier by technological advancement in communication and transportation, and the opportunity becomes accessible to a much larger number of students. On the other hand, the weakened boundaries between nations and the pressure to converge in an increasingly globalized world make it more difficult and thus more important to maintain one's heritage and identity. As a result, students studying overseas may become more easily confused about their identity in the face of conflicted perspectives and values. In this sense, the dilemma facing those students may be the age-old one: How does one bridge two totally different worlds without becoming "patriots and traitors, heroes and villains, and vanguard and scapegoat" all at the same time?

References

Bevis, T. B., & Lucas, C. J. (2007). *International students in American colleges and universities: A history*. New York, NY: Palgrave Macmillan.

Bieler, S. (2004). *"Patriots" or "traitors"? A history of American-educated Chinese students*. New York, NY: M. E. Sharpe.

Caldwell, O. J. (1965). Education comes of age around the world. In S. Frazer (Ed.), *Governmental policy and international education*. New York, NY: John Wiley & Sons.

Chen, J. (1997). Western learning and social transmutation in the late Qing. In F. Wakeman Jr. & W. Xi (Eds.), *China's Quest for Modernization: A historical perspective*. Berkeley, CA: University of California Press.

Ding, R. (1997). Dowager empress Cixi and Toshimichi: A comparative study of modernization in China and Japan. In F. Wakeman Jr. & W. Xi (Eds.), *China's Quest for Modernization: A historical perspective*. Berkeley, CA: University of California Press.

Dong, M. (2003). On foreign students who came to study in ancient China. *Overseas Chinese Education, 26*(1), 68–74.

Du Bois, C. (1956). *Foreign students and higher education in the United States*. Washington, DC: American Council on Education.

Harrell, P. (1992). *Sowing the seeds of change: Chinese students, Japanese teachers, 1895–1905*. Stanford, CA: Stanford University Press.

LaFargue, T. E. (1987). *China's first hundred: Educational mission students in the United States, 1872–1881*. Pullman, WA: Washington State University Press.

Leibovitz, L., & Miller, M. (2011). *Fortunate Sons: The 120 Chinese boys who came to America, went to school, and revolutionized an ancient civilization*. New York, NY: W. W. Norton & Company.

Li, H. (2008). *U.S.-China educational exchange: State, society, and intercultural relations, 1905–1950*. New Brunswick, NJ: Rutgers University Press.

Lin, R. V. (2016). Eastward Expansion of Western Learning: A study of Westernisation of China's modern education by Chinese government overseas-study scholarship. *Educational Philosophy and Theory, 48*(12), 1203–1207.

Lum, Y., & Lum, R. (1999). *Sun Yat-sen in Hawaii: Activities and supporters*. Honolulu, HI: Hawaii Chinese History Center.

Luo, R. (1997). A new approach to China's century of great transformation, 1840s–1940s. In F. Wakeman Jr. & W. Xi (Eds.), *China's Quest for Modernization: A historical perspective*. Berkeley, CA: University of California Press.

Ministry of Education. (2019). *Statistics on Chinese students who went abroad in 2018*. Retrieved from http://www.moe.gov.cn/jyb_xwfb/gzdt_gzdt/s5987/201903/t20190327_375704.html

Walden, J. W. H. (1909). *The universities of ancient Greece*. New York: Charles Scribner's Sons.

Wang, C. (2013). *Transpacific articulations: Student migration and the remaking of Asian America*. Honolulu, HI: University of Hawaii Press.

Wang, X. (1997). Approaches to the study of modern Chinese history: External versus internal causations. In F. Wakeman Jr. & W. Xi (Eds.), *China's Quest for Modernization: A historical perspective*. Berkeley, CA: University of California Press.

Ye, W. (2001). *Seeking modernity in China's name: Chinese students in the United States, 1900–1927*. Stanford, CA: Stanford University Press.

Yung, W. (1909). *My life in China and America*. Originally published by New York Henry Hold Company, transcribed by Cassandra Bates in 2006.

Chapter 3
An Overview of China's Education

Introduction

To understand the characteristics of education in China, we need to have a panoramic understanding. Therefore, this chapter first introduces the scale and quality development of education system and summarizes the achievements of contemporary education in China, the differences between private education and public education, and the challenges faced. Among the many characteristics of Chinese education, "international reform" is the key word of this chapter. This chapter focuses on various international activities carried out by schools in K-12 education in China, including internationalization of competence model, courses, teaching methods, and academic evaluation standards. However, different types of schools have various motivation and development process of internationalized reform, so this chapter analyzes the internationalization reform path of public schools and private schools respectively. Through analysis, we find that in K-12 education in China, "internationalization" is reflected in curriculum integration, teacher growth, student development, and other aspects, which is consistent with China's economic and social development strategy "opening up," and will have a significant impact on China's education development.

© Springer Nature Singapore Pte Ltd. 2020   41
B. Cheng et al., *The New Journey to the West*, Education in the Asia-Pacific
Region: Issues, Concerns and Prospects 53,
https://doi.org/10.1007/978-981-15-5588-6_3

An Overview of the Scale and Quality of China's Education

The Proportion and Scale of Education at Each Level

China is not only a country with a large population; it is also a strong education market. According to China Statistical Yearbook (2016),[1] China had a population of 1.37 billion at the end of 2015, with a domestic GDP of 6.856 billion yuan and a GDP of 50,000 yuan per capita, equivalent to nearly 7000 US dollars. After several years of hard work, China has primarily made compulsory free education a common luxury, so that all children aged 6–15 in every provinces and place can enjoy their 6 years of primary and 3 years of secondary education free of charge. According to the Statistical Bulletin of Education in China (2016)[2] issued by the Chinese Ministry of Education, there are 177,600 elementary schools nationwide with 17,524,700 new enrollments, 99,130,100 students currently studying in schools and 15,047,500 graduates. The net enrollment rate of primary school-age children reaches 99.92%. A total of 52,100 junior middle schools nationwide (including 16 vocational junior high schools) with 43,293,700 students, with 14,871,700 newly enrolled students, and 14,238,700 graduates. The gross enrollment rate in junior high schools is 104.0% and its graduation rate is 93.7%. At present, the free education policy may be extended to include early childhood education, as well as senior high school education.

In China, senior high school is non-compulsory and not every student is forced to continue. Meanwhile, a career aspect is introduced in the senior level; therefore, high schools in China are divided into general education high schools and vocational high schools. There are 24,700 high schools national wide with 13,962,600 students enrolled, making a total of 39,701,600 students, having a drop of 667,300 comparing with the number in 2015. The gross enrollment ratio in high school was 87.5%, which is an increase of 0.5 percentage points from 2016. The overall trend of high school students is declining, with increases mainly occurring in general education senior high schools, while the number of students in various vocational senior high schools, vocational junior high schools, and secondary technical schools are continuously decreasing. There are 1340 general education high schools across the country, showing an increase of 143 throughout 2015; with 8,029,200 new student enrollments (an increase of 63,100 over 2015). There was a total of 23,666,500 students enrolled in high school, which was 775,000 less than the previous year. Student graduates were 53,000 lower than the previous year with a total of 7.9235 million graduates. General high school students accounted for 59.6% of the total number of high school students, while vocational high schools accounted for 40.4%. Students from both these two types of high schools can enter the university through college entrance examination, but generally speaking vocational high school graduates will mainly choose to enter the higher vocational colleges. In addition, general

---

[1] http://www.stats.gov.cn/tjsj/ndsj/

[2] http://www.moe.edu.cn/jyb_sjzl/sjzl_fztjgb/201707/t20170710_309042.html

high school students who pass the college entrance examination can choose to enter both the general college and higher vocational college to pursue further study.

In China, the total number of students receiving various types of higher education has reached 36.99 million, and the gross enrollment rate is 42.7%. At the same time, the number of colleges and enrollment scale show a rising trend. In 2016, there was a total of 2880 general institutions of higher education and adult higher education institutions nationwide; an increase of 28 from 2015. Among them, there are 2596 general institutions of higher education (including 266 independent colleges) which is an increase of 36 over 2015; and 284 adult institutions of higher education which is a decrease of 8 over 2015. Along the general institutions of higher education, there are 1237 undergraduate colleges and universities; hence, an increase of 18 from 2015; and 1359 higher vocational and technical colleges and universities, having an increase of 18 from 2015. There are altogether 793 postgraduate institutions nationwide, of which 576 are general colleges and universities, and 217 are scientific research institutions.

Here, we are more concerned about the colleges and universities' admission opportunities. The total enrollment in general higher education is 7.4861 million, having an increase of 107,600 compared with 2015, which consists of 26,958,400 students in school (705,500 more than 2015) and 704.18 million graduates, which has increased by 232,900 compared to the previous year. Although the gross domestic enrollment rate in China's higher education has reached 42.7%, it is still unsatisfactory considering the huge population base and strong demand for higher education. Therefore, on the one hand, higher education institutions continue to grow in terms of the number of schools and number of enrollments; on the other hand, the enrollment demand for higher education is not limited to institutions within China, with more and more students are seeking ways to study abroad. The number of new overseas students studying abroad in China reached 544,500 in 2016.[3] Furthermore, according to OECD's estimation, there were five million students studying overseas in 2015, with Chinese students accounting for one tenth of the total number of students studying abroad. As China's reform becomes deeper and continues to open up, the improvement of the per capita income level of Chinese people, as well the impact of the economic globalization, will provide much more space for further growth and possibilities in the future.

The Stratification and Selection of Education in China

Although the overall size of the education market in China is already very large, and the industry has made great strides through the universalization of compulsory education and the development of higher education, imbalance remains as a prominent feature of China's education. Part of this is due to the vast territory of China, and

---

[3] http://www.stats.gov.cn/tjsj/ndsj/

hence there are differences in the economic development and cultural traditions among various regions. The central finance system uses transfer payments to balance the financial resources of various regions and to guarantee the development of the relatively undeveloped areas. However, the main policy of funds for basic education is still counter-based under the co-ordination of provincial governments.[4] This means that while the minimum standards for spending on basic education are safeguarded, there are still great regional differences in quality education resources. There is a fivefold difference in government and families' spending on education in the eastern and western regions of China, which means that there is most likely significant differences in the education quality, facilities, and equipment, between those regions;[5] not only is this difference clear between the eastern and western, it is even obvious within the same province. The developed capital cities and the underdeveloped townships cannot be simply compared by their quality and level of their education.

The stratification of education in China means the scarcity of high-quality educational resources. In order for families to give their children access to quality education resources, competition among different social levels has been created. This competition runs throughout the education process: starting from the fight for admission opportunities into key primary schools, middle schools, senior high schools, all the way to major universities. Competition means screening: limited access to quality educational resources and scarce education admission opportunities means that suppliers need to set barriers in order screen those applying. There are two types of screening to filter out students: economic screening and ability screening. Economic screening means that some high-quality educational resources will be rejected by applicants due to the pricing. The mechanisms of economic and ability screening are particularly evident in all stages of both compulsory and non-compulsory education, as well as in the fields of school education and after-school education. Especially in the stage of compulsory education, even though all school-age children can enjoy free education resources and receive education of a certain quality standard, not all age-appropriate children have access to high school and only about 40% of students have access to non-vocational high schools since the upper-level education, i.e., high school education is a scarce resource. In the perceptions of most Chinese parents, good academic performance means a better future. In addition, they perceive technology-related education as a low level of schooling and academic education related to general knowledge as a higher level of schooling, which is closely related to the common cultural tradition "emphasis on methods rather than application techniques" which is prominent within East Asian countries.

---

[4]Yuan (2011).

[5]http://www.moe.edu.cn/srcsite/A05/s3040/201710/t20171025_317429.html. According to *2016 National Education Fund Implementation Statistics Bulletin* by Ministry of education, National Bureau of Statistics, and the Ministry of Finance, in 2016, the administrative area with the highest average cost of public finance budget education is Beijing, among which the average cost of primary school is 25,793.55 yuan, while in the lowest Henan province, this indicator is only 5038.31 yuan.

Therefore, general high schools which mainly teach the general knowledge of subjects are widely favored by parents and students, which form the two main types for the screening and competition of high school enrollment. There is also obvious differentiation of screening even within ordinary high schools: not all high school students are allowed to enter key universities. Most of the major universities' students have graduated from key high schools. Therefore, students in the compulsory education stage are required to focus on competing for admissions into key high schools first, in order to obtain possible entrance into key universities.

In China, students who finished a three-year junior high school are required to take an entrance examination in order to enter high school to continue their studies for another 3 years, which is somewhat equivalent to the examination American students take after grade 9, before they reach the 10th grade. The exam is called the Senior High School Test in China. It is a level test that examines whether middle-school students have reached junior middle-school standard, and it also acts as selection criteria for high schools based on the 9 years of compulsory education. Therefore, it is necessary for students to take this exam to obtain their junior high school diploma. All the subjects specified in the national curriculum will be included in the test. Students can apply for the corresponding general high schools, vocational high schools, and technical secondary schools according to the results of the test. However, most students will initially apply for a general high school. The Senior High School Entrance Examination has to consider the capability and potential of junior high school graduates; however, the high school education itself still falls under the category of foundational education. Therefore, the test must not only include the examination of basic knowledge, methods, and skills, but also insist on examining the academic ability. The examination is usually organized by the provincial administrative department to carry out unified question topics, examination, and admission.

After the third year of high school, equivalent to after the 12th grade in the United States, there is a larger nationwide examination, namely, the National College Entrance Examination, which is abbreviated as *Gaokao* in China. It is an examination used for the selection of qualified high school graduates and equivalent candidates in China (excluding Hong Kong, Macau, and Taiwan). Differentiating from the senior high school entrance examination, *Gaokao* combines the functions of both academic qualifications evaluation and university selection examinations. It is held annually from June 7–9 by provinces with their own unified organization and set of questions. All types of higher education institutions at various levels in China organize college admission within 2 months of July and August each year, according to the allocation regulations set by each province. As the college entrance examination is the examination which is the most attended, most emphasized, and receives the most public attention and concern, academic research on the college entrance examination has become abundant, from the scientific proposition, to the unification of the examination, to the fairness of admission, and so on. More importantly, because of the stratification of Chinese universities, most of the universities rely solely on the scores of college entrance examination to screen candidates for admission in order to maintain the equality. As a result, a score difference of one point may accumulate thousands of candidates, leading to pursuing scores to be accurate to two decimal places or even three. The micro-difference in scores, which creates huge differences in admission opportunities, leads candidates and parents haggle over every test point. In order to gain some advantage in the college entrance examination, grade 12 students spend almost one whole year training repetitively on various topics, posing a heavy burden on students. In China, there is an image metaphor which the majority of parents and candidates have for the college entrance examination: a mighty force of thousands upon thousands of soldiers and horse crossing a single-plank bridge. 20 years ago, the college entrance examination was a qualifier as to whether or not a student can go to college, then 20 years later, the college entrance examination became a competition to get into a good university. The Ministry of Education of China has started the reform of college entrance examination and enrollment in Shanghai and Zhejiang provinces in 2014, which is aimed at breaking the "one-time test" and giving students more chances, so that college admission does not only depend on the score, but also the comprehensive quality of students. Although in 2017, high school students from the two places have completed their exams under the new test and admission system. Although such a system is in practice, it has also encountered many problems. Multiple examinations still place burdens upon students. Parents and teachers' confusion of the new college entrance examination system creates problems within the biggest interest groups of this education chain.

Even though the college entrance examination reform is advancing, for most provinces and cities, Chinese parents and students still inherent impressions of the former college entrance examination, as well as the reality of relative scarcity of China's high-quality higher education institutions, it still takes time to reverse all exam-oriented education, teaching methods, counseling, and exam preparation. Therefore, many students and parents, especially those with advantages in aspects of social relations, economic status, and expertise, have been trying to find other ways beyond the narrow passage of the college entrance examination.[6] Studying abroad is undoubtedly a good choice. Globalization and new internet technologies have further reduced the cost of cross-border mobility and exchange of information, and as the admission opportunities abroad progressively gain recognition and acceptance by their parents and students in China, they have generated their demands in this regard. On the other hand, China being a huge market is not only recognized in the economic field but also in the field of education. Chinese parents and students' enthusiasm for private investment in education has brought hope to some colleges and universities who have an allotted funding crisis due to the decrease in their source of students and a reduction in federal funding, as well as the given tremendous opportunities for education in international exchange to countries as Britain and Australia that regard higher education as a business enterprise. The British and Australian governments have not only promoted cultural exchange programs with

---

[6] Fan and Cheng (2018).

China, but also guided and helped Chinese students study abroad in their country as an important diplomatic mission and government responsibility.[7]

The Contrast of Public Education and Private Education

Formal school system in China is dominated by public education; and therefore just the same as public schools, private education has huge stratification too. A large portion of private education in China is set up to meet the unmet needs of the public system because of the lack of resources, typically schools for migrant worker's children. These private schools provide schooling opportunities for children who have migrated with their parents from rural areas to urban areas who cannot enter the local schools in the urban districts. Besides this, the private schools satisfy some of the other differential demands that the public system cannot meet. For example, private bilingual schools provide Chinese students with similar curriculum to those in English-speaking countries such as the United States, Britain, Canada, and Australia, for them to gain better academic preparation for studying in universities in these countries. Private schools for migrant children tend to charge low fees with poor teaching quality, which can only provide students with basic discipline and the minimum curriculum, while private international schools, which teach both in Chinses and English, tend to be expensive, putting more emphasis on the personal experience of students and parents' satisfaction, as well as they pay more attention to the future progress of students' studies abroad. Private international schools are the main body of current internationalized schooling. The schools gained strong momentum in their development and received a great deal of financial support, becoming an important direction for the development of Chinese private schooling, and possibly an important growth point for Chinese private schools. For example, The China Bright Scholar (*Boshile*) Education Group, which is listed in the United States, is an education group that owns a number of privately run international schools in China.

Generally speaking, private education follows the path of differentiated development, among which internationalization is one of the more distinctive and meaningful aspects. Of course, private school education is an important core of private education, but the scope of private education in China is broader and not limited to it. Similar to the extensive tutoring culture in East Asia, there are a large number of off-campus training schools in China that are independent of the school education system and provide post-school knowledge and interest development for students. It is like the shadow of the school education, always going with the normal school education system. And the more quality schools the students from, the greater the percentage of all types of tutoring they receive. The interesting thing is that, two of the top education-type companies in China listed in the United States are both

---

[7] https://www.iie.org/Research-and-Insights/Open-Doors

training schools, namely "New Oriental" and "Good Future." Among them, "New Oriental" is an out-of-school training company focusing on language classes for overseas study. The successful development of "New Oriental" undoubtedly verifies that studying abroad and internationalization are an important direction for China's education needs and also an important field of the private education investments.

The story of the capital market reveals that many of the developments in private education in China are integrated with internationalization. If there is no development direction of internationalization, it is impossible to notice the achievement of two billion-level education listed companies with market capital. Such stories continue to inspire Chinese investors and private school operators, and both training institutions of overseas study and languages or private schools engaged in the traditional Gaokao-oriented teaching method have held an international school as their own investment goals. Under the impetus of such capital power, basic education in China, especially that of private education, has continued to grow and develop. Objectively speaking, it has provided people with more optional international education services and products, and further promoted and guided public awareness and willingness to study abroad.

The Internationalized Reform of Basic Education in China

There is no consensus on the internationalization of China's basic education. The so-called internationalization here is essentially the degree of similarity between the 12-year education of primary, middle, and high school in China, and that of advanced English-speaking countries such as the United States, Canada, and Britain in terms of curriculum, teaching, and promotion. That is to say, there are differences in similarities from school to school. For example, some public schools with low similarities increase their international and intercollegiate exchanges through the establishment of partner schools and learn from their K-12 education in terms of teaching experience; there are also schools with high similarities, such as schools for foreign children, being a comprehensive model of the primary and secondary schools in these countries including the enrollment, curriculum, and operations management, with the only main difference being that they are located in China. Therefore, internationalization is a concept with varying levels. At the same time, while further strengthening international exchanges, China's K-12 education places special emphasis on the concept of integrated curriculums. Its purpose is to integrate foreign advanced teaching methods and contents on the basis of Chinese local culture. Therefore, the internationalization of China's basic education consists of three aspects. The first is the integration of educational philosophy and goals with the aim of international personnel training. The second is the internationalization of curriculum content, teaching methods, and academic evaluation standards. The third is the internationalization from the perspective of students' studying abroad and the interaction with higher level education institutes in foreign countries.

The concept of education and training objectives relates to the sovereignty of a country and the value of national citizens. Therefore, it has always been highly valued by the government. Thus, the direction of China's K-12 education reform is not "internationalization" or "foreignization," but integration and innovation while still maintaining Chinese traditional culture and current social values. Whether it is China's national curriculum or IB course, or a secondary school curriculum from the United Kingdom, the United States, or Canada, there are many similarities in the cultivation of people, which is the basis for the exchange, usage, and integration of different countries' curriculum systems. Through a large amount of literature analysis, experts in China's K-12 education reform defined, selected, implemented, and developed students' core qualities which use reference from three international organizations (OECD, UNESCO, and the European Union), ten countries including the United States, Canada, the United Kingdom, France, Finland, Hungary, Australia, New Zealand, Japan and Singapore and two special autonomous regions such as Taiwan, and Hong Kong. They refined the future needs of Chinese students' core academic skills which include: communication, teamwork, information literacy, innovative literacy, social participation and contribution, self-planning and self-management, international perspective, language literacy, mathematical literacy, learning capability, problem solving. At the same time, these experts systematically classify the traditional Chinese culture and schools of thought, based on more than 30 representative works from important thinkers and schools of historical periods from the pre-Qin period to the Qing Dynasty, as well as nearly 100 books and essays from modern and contemporary scholars. They then analyze these texts and elaborated on Chinese students' values including benevolence and love, cherishing the world, contributing to society, filial piety and patriotism, nationalism, native emotion, honesty, and self-discipline. On the third aspect, the experts conducted a standard analysis on the content of core literature in current curriculums and adopted content analysis methods to encode and classify texts into 19 curricular standards in compulsory education and 16 curricula in high school education. They then obtained the content and frequency of the core literature contained in the four parts: prefaces, curriculum objectives, curriculum contents, and implementation suggestions of the 35 current curricular standards. The study shows that the core qualities of students' development include the following aspects: learning literacy, language literacy, scientific literacy, art and esthetic literacy, practical literacy, communication and communication, active inquiry, information literacy, humanistic literacy, and problem solving. They combine international comparison with traditional cultural analysis and curriculum standards analysis, etc. and put forward the core of training of students in basic education in China is "all-round development of human," which can be divided into cultural basis, independent development, social participation, and its overall performance is the six qualities of humanities and cultural heritage, the spirit of science, learning capability, healthy living, responsibility, and innovation practicing. From the refinement of core literacy in China's basic education to its substantive connotation, we can all see the fit between the standard of personnel training in basic education in China and that of international personnel training.

Second, in teaching methods and academic evaluation, the internationalization of China's basic education is mainly reflected in the frequent exchange, visits, and communication between schools and local educational institutions with foreign primary and secondary schools. This communication includes management level, teacher level, and student level. Its promotion of internationalization incorporates the educational administration departments and relevant institutions at the district level, the groups and alliances of single school or schools level, and the possible spontaneous participation of students. For example, the Education Commission of Chaoyang District, Beijing, as a local administrative department, has taken internationalization as a direction and characteristic of its development of local basic education. They rely on Chaoyang Education Institute to invite foreign teachers to Beijing to visit and teach local primary and secondary school teachers, as well as how to carry out project-based teaching and inquiry-based learning. They hope that such training and communication will broaden teachers' horizons and enhance teachers' teaching level, so they can be able to absorb and take international advanced teaching methods. Such communication led by local school districts and educational administration departments are included at the management level, which is the principal level, and also embraces the teacher level. Schools are also provided more chances in international exchanges and communication opportunities of teachers and students with foreign schools through establishing cooperation with foreign schools and increasing school-level exchanges. Of course, these attempts mainly occur in public and private schools in economically developed areas. In terms of teaching evaluation, Shanghai took part in PISA on behalf of China in 2013 and achieved good results in 65 participating countries and regions. This has also led the international education community to pay attention to the basic education and the academic development of students in China. It also shows the dialogues and comparisons between the achievements of China's basic education and those of other countries.

Thirdly, some public and private schools try to establish a large number of projects conducting students to studying abroad. This is one of the most notable topics in the field of internationalizing basic education in China—International Schools. China's international schools can be broadly divided into three categories: schools for foreign children, public international schools, and the private international schools. The element which these three schools have in common is the higher potential for their students to enter foreign high schools or universities for further study. Due to their direction to send graduates abroad, their internationalization holds too main aspects: their cultivating ideas and teaching methods are very similar to foreign primary and secondary schools. The main difference is that schools for foreign children are run directly by various types of foreign institutions and legal foreign residents in order to provide diploma courses that can be used internationally. Under Chinese law, foreign children's schools can only admit non-Chinese nationality students. Private international schools refer to private schools that adopt Chinese students as their main enrollment targets and partly employ take part or all of the overseas curriculum system, teaching materials, and test evaluation. Overseas courses in these schools are mainly taught in English. International classes in public schools are international education programs run by Chinese public schools (usually public high schools) in cooperation with foreign schools. The Chinese public schools teaching is managed according to overseas teaching plan, syllabus, teaching materials, and test evaluation; and they adopt bilingual or English teaching methods to cultivate international academic skills. The international departments of public schools and private international schools mainly enroll Chinese students. According to incomplete statistics, in 2017, there are 126 foreign children's schools in China, 241 international departments in public schools, and 367 private international schools. In the recent 3 years, the number of foreign children's schools and public schools' international department has grown slowly by not more than 20 in 2 years, while the privately run international school has enjoyed a very rapid growth of more than 100 during the 2 years. The following two sections of this chapter will focus on the international department of public schools and private international schools in the aspects of internationalization reform of public schools and the international development of private schools.

The Internationalized Reform of Public Schools

China's public schools occupy an absolutely dominant position in the entire basic education system. According to *Statistical Bulletin of Education in 2016*, there are about 165 million students from grades 1–12 in the whole country, of which public school students make up more than 75%. In public schools, the majority of students are aiming to progress all the way through the domestic education system. However, in order to broaden their horizons, schools may organize short-term study tours (1 week to 2 months) in the summer to help them obtain short-term visits and study in primary schools or even universities abroad. Most of the study tours organized by these schools are based on the establishment of partner schools between public schools and some primary and secondary schools abroad. Some schools organize and carry out these trips with the help of middleman agencies. These tours are usually led by teachers in the public school, and teachers from both schools can also learn from each other during the visits. The cost of these trips is usually paid by students themselves.

In addition to the international communication among students and teachers, some key schools and high-quality schools have also achieved various degrees of internationalization by a number of different ways. There are two main ways: the first is by the introduction of foreign teachers, and the second is to send local teachers to study abroad or attend training. In former practices, foreign teachers were introduced usually as to act as linguistic teachers. These teachers usually had teaching qualifications and were mainly engaged in language teaching activities. This method was used only in key schools of first-tier cities with a developed economy. In contrast, for those common primary and secondary schools, foreign teachers are too costly and it's difficult to attract them to work in unrenowned schools. The latter method is more common, which is to train local teachers with teaching methods and other aspects at foreign countries or by experts from abroad. This is usually organized by the regional education administrative departments, education groups, or with union organizations and can provide a window for the professional development of local teachers.

Regardless of the students' trips abroad during their vacation, or the cross-border training of teachers and the employment of foreign teachers from overseas, these factors are all part of the internationalization of public school education process, and there is no direct connection with students' choice to go abroad and to take further education. The international department of public schools is a teaching organization which was developed in response to the students' needs in the public education system. Public school international department underwent a certain course of development.

The First Phase (2000–2005): Beginning

Since the late 1990s, there has been a new wave of Chinese students studying overseas, a trend which led to the dramatic increase in students pursuing undergraduate studies in Britain, Canada, and Australia. After 2000, some overseas study agents started trying to introduce overseas preparation courses and set up cooperation with domestic university abroad to set up preparatory study centers under the name of local schools. This opened the beginning of China hosting international courses in local schools. Some representative institutions of these kind of centers include ACE and NCUK (later bought by Kaplan).

By the end of 2001, China joined the WTO. In accordance with the promise of opening up to the education service industry, the ministry of education propagated the *Sino-Foreign Cooperative Education Regulations* in 2003 and the *Measures for the Implementation of the Regulations on Sino-Foreign Cooperation in Qualifying Schools* in 2004, establishing a legal basis for setting up international education programs in local schools. In the compulsory education stage, high schools are allowed to set up Sino-foreign cooperative education programs as a way to set up an international curriculum. Since then, domestic educational exchange agencies and educational intermediaries began to introduce foreign curricula to local Chinese schools, as well as beginning an active exploration into the internationalization of local schools; with public schools such as the High School Affiliated to Renmin University of China and private schools such as Beijing's Royal School, Shenzhen College of International Education, as well as Beijing Huijia Private School are all key schools which belonged to the first batch of excellent local schools which have introduced international curricula. During this period, the majority of schools chose to use curricula from the United Kingdom, Canada, and Australia.

The Second Phase (2005–2013): Rapid Development

During the next stage, the international education programs organized by public schools have been rapidly developed. At the same time, CIE, CB, IBO, and other international curriculum certification systems were gradually introduced into various schools. The number of schools and projects' growth was the fastest following the education movement for local schools attempting to internationalize their education. Since the 9 year of compulsory education does not allow the full introduction of an overseas education system, the rapid growth international schools during this stage was still mainly prominent in senior high schools.

Besides the pressure created by high demand, The Public School International Department being the supplier, also has wide-ranging motives: on the one hand, schools can charge a higher fee than that of an ordinary high school for offering related courses and providing teachers with better benefits, hence giving schools a great incentive; on the other hand, the preparation and application time for students who plan to study abroad is not consistent with that of the college entrance examination. In the second semester of Grade 12, students studying abroad may have already received the admission notice in university while others are entering the intense preparation for Chinese College Entrance Exam (Gaokao). With the two different directions of higher study, the learning rhythm and mood of both the students gathering together may have a serious effect on students' college entrance exam preparation. Therefore, in order to manage this, schools usually separate the students going to study abroad and organize separate academic and application preparation.

The Third Stage (After 2013): Policy Construction

In 2012, the Ministry of Education began to pay close attention to the phenomenon of large-scale international education projects taken by local students and started policy research and investigation into the matter. Local governments began to cautiously examine or stop some projects. The international classes held by high schools all over the country were set up to be more like "curriculum reform experimental classes" which were set up by the schools own "international department." However due to the lack of a unified supervision system, there is not yet a very accurate official statistics available.

In 2013, the Ministry of Education made it clear that all forms of high school "international department" and "international class" will be regulated and the government has ordered to inspect and count all Sino-foreign cooperative education projects in each region.

In May 2013, the Shanghai Education Commission issued the *Notice on Developing General International Curricula of High School* (Shanghai Education Commission [2013] No. 37), explicitly introducing the value orientation of international curricula, as well as regulating the practice and management of introducing international curricula into regular senior high schools. A total 21 experimental schools were established on the premise of strict examination and quality assurance. These 21 high schools can provide high school students in Shanghai with an "integrated" form of international curriculum education and teaching methods.

Following the introduction of the Standardized International Class Policies in Shanghai and other regions, the Beijing Municipal Education Commission also strengthened the scale of enrollment in international high schools in 2014, and no longer approved new high school to embark in Sino-foreign cooperative education programs. The official website of Beijing Municipal Education Commission has released the *List of Sino-foreign Cooperation Established Schools in Beijing* with a total of 26 existing projects.

In addition, both Hangzhou and Ningbo in Zhejiang Province have established certain regulations regarding the enrollment of public international students in high schools by stipulating the policy that students planning to participate in international projects need to take the senior high school entrance examination first. In October 2016, the Beijing Municipal Commission of Education and Beijing Municipal Bureau of Finance released the *Guide for the Major Budgetary Inputs and Projects of the Education Sector in Beijing in 2018,* proposing to "support the transformation of the international department of urban high schools." In future, when this policy is implemented, the international department of public schools is likely to be implicated by policies and their further development may be limited.

Although the international department of public schools has been criticized for using up public education resources, it has been objectively recognized by many parents and foreign well-known colleges and universities because of its lower fees compared to privately run international schools, quality assurance, and large number of enrollments. In some schools, the international department has also become an experimental field for course innovation. With outstanding achievements of education and teaching, the international department has nurtured the development and reform of the curriculum used in schools and played a particular role in promoting the international development of public schools as a whole.

The Internationalized Reform of Private Schools

Following the methods mentioned above, private schools are undoubtedly an important force in the internationalization of China's K-12 education. China's K-12 education internalization is not only characterized by its exponential growth and rapid development, but also by its degree of internationalization in hardware facilities, curricula, organization management, and promotion. These factors have always been higher than that of public schools from the very beginning. During the period of 1995–2000 was when private schools initially attempted to explore internationalization. Starting from the *Regulations on the Establishing Schools for Social Services* in the late 1990s to the *Law on Promotion of Private Education* which was promulgated in 2003, all the policies demonstrate the government's attitude in encouraging the development of privately run education. During this period, various modes of operation emerged with enterprise-established school, public-assistance school, local–private schools, and public school transformations being the main types of private schools. At the beginning of their development, many non-governmental schools had already begun their attempts to internationalize, taking advantage of the relatively open policies for state supervision and management. For example, Beijing World Youth Academy, Beijing International Bilingual Academy (Haijia), Beijing Huijia Private School, Beijing Royal School, and several others introduced international courses right from the founding of their schools. Some schools introduce high-quality international curricula by establishing overseas departments, international departments, and bilingual classes. Some examples include Shanghai World Foreign Language Middle School, Shanghai Pinghe Bilingual School, and many others. However, during the next 5 years (2005–2010), due to the explosive growth of public international school curriculum projects, private schools became not as superior in terms of enrollment fees, reputation, quality of students, and international education resources as those key public schools who had set up international programs. Therefore, the development of private schools has slowed down.

However, with the international department of public schools facing abolishment after the policies introduced in 2013 and the strong demand for international schools, it ushered new developments in private international school. Despite studying at a younger age becoming a growing trend, many parents are also aware that sending their children abroad between grade 9 and 12 or even lower grades may lead to children facing many psychological, security, and learning difficulties. "Studying abroad locally," which means to enjoy international education service without ever going abroad is undoubtedly the best choice for them. Therefore, in some large cities, high-quality private international schools are even more difficult to get access to. The enrollment rate of bilingual classes at outstanding private international schools in Beijing and Shanghai is on average more than 9:1. The penetration of private schools in China's overall K-12 education sector (based on enrollment) rose. At the same time, private international schools, especially primary schools and junior high schools that were founded earlier, were gradually sought after by local parents and students. Related industries and capital investments received huge dividends, and many investors and entrepreneurs started entering the privately run international school market, hoping to gain a share from it. In the past, overseas study intermediaries, extracurricular training schools, and traditional private schools all marched toward internationalization. In China, internationalization has become an important direction for the pursuit of differentiated development in private schools. More importantly, Chinese parents and students in these environments are increasingly accepting international education, and studying abroad is no longer a choice for the minorities, but an educational option that can be considered by a growing majority of families.

References

China Statistical Yearbook. (2016). Retrieved from http://www.stats.gov.cn/tjsj/ndsj/

Fan, A., & Cheng, B. (2018). Social stratification and studying overseas: Empirical evidence from middle schools in Beijing. *The Asia-Pacific Education Researcher, 27*, 11–21.

Statistical Bulletin of Education in China. (2016). Retrieved from http://www.moe.edu.cn/jyb_sjzl/sjzl_fztjgb/201707/t20170710_309042.html

Yuan, L. (2011). Characteristics of China's education finance system and its assessment. *Journal of Beijing Normal University, 5*, 10–16.

Chapter 4
Chinese High School Students' Plans in Studying Overseas: Who and Why

Introduction

This chapter aims to provide evidence well-grounded in empirical research to address the questions of who in current China plans to study overseas and why they would like to study overseas. The goal is to better understand the driving force behind the largest outflow of international students from China. It is the first study employing large-scale data to thoroughly examine factors affecting Chinese students' motives and decision-making in studying overseas and how those factors are related to students' family socioeconomic status (SES). The data were collected from 18 high schools in the three cities of Beijing, Chengdu, and Shenzhen, between the summer of 2015 and the summer of 2016.

International Student Mobility and Institutional Motives

The direction in which international students flow is uneven, mostly from developing, non-English-speaking countries in the East such as China and India to developed, English-speaking countries in the West such as the United States, the United Kingdom, and Australia (Perkins & Neumayer, 2014). In 2014, among the 4.5 million international students worldwide, about 53% are from Asia, and in Asia the top three sending countries of international students are China, India, and Korea (OECD, 2015). As Altbach and Knight (2007) pointed out: "International academic mobility … favors well-developed education systems and institutions, thereby

---

An earlier version of this chapter was published as the following journal article:
Cheng, B., Fan, A., Liu, M. (2017). Chinese High School Student's Plans in Studying Overseas: Who and Why. *Frontiers of Education in China*, *12*(3), 367–393.

compounding existing inequalities" (p. 291). However, starting around the mid-1990s the dominating position of English-speaking countries like the United States, the United Kingdom, and Australia as traditional popular destination for international students have been challenged, and new directions for student mobility have emerged: by the early 2010s some Asian countries such as China, Singapore, and Malaysia had become competitive destinations for foreign students (Knight, 2011; Tan, 2013).

It is widely recognized that receiving and educating international students has multiple benefits, including adding diversity to the student body, providing students in host countries with the first close contact they have with a person from another culture, filling the under-enrolled courses that colleges would otherwise find it difficult to offer and providing crucial support as teaching and research assistants, especially in the sciences (Bartlett & Fischer, 2011; Johnson, 2003; Rogers, 1984). However, there is no denying that financial consideration is an important factor in recruiting international students. In the majority of countries where data are available, international students pay higher tuition fees at public educational institutions than do national students enrolled in the same program. For example, in the United States, at public institutions international students are usually charged out-of-state tuition fees which are considerably higher than in-state tuition fees. In Austria, students enrolled at public institutions who are not citizens of the European Union or European Economic Area countries are usually charged twice as much in tuition fees as citizens of those countries. Similar policies of differential charges based on an individual's citizenship or residence can be found in countries such as the United Kingdom, Canada, and New Zealand (OECD, 2014). In fact, Throsby (1986), who analyzed the Australian fee-charging policies toward foreign students in tertiary education from an economic perspective about three decades ago, supported the proposals to introduce a full economic fee for foreign students. Kinnell (1989) indicated that higher education institution in the United Kingdom, the United States, and Australia adopted a marketing approach in recruiting international students because of the pressure to generate revenues.

Financial incentives for recruiting international students have become more important in recent years. As educational institutions face an increasingly restrained budget situation after the 2008 financial crisis, many of them turn to the tremendous international student market for a solution. International education is a huge business indeed. For example, it is reported that higher education has become an important export product for the United States and ranks No. 5 in the service industry (Li & Zhang, 2011). In Australia, the total national exports of higher education, vocational education, schooling, and English-language courses were AUD ten million in 2009, and education had become the nation's largest services export and fourth largest export after coal, iron ore, and gold, ahead of tourism, agriculture, and manufacturing (Marginson, 2011). The annual report *Open Doors* estimated that in 2015–16, international students had contributed $32.8 billion and 400,000 jobs to the US economy (IIE, 2016).

   Given the multiple benefits of having international students, it is no surprise that nations compete against each other to attract international students (Knight, 2011). Therefore, it has become a priority for institutions and policy-makers to understand students' motives and decision-making in studying abroad.

Push-and-Pull Factors

Studies have long existed examining factors related to international student mobility. Having guided researchers in migration for many years (Ravenstein, 1885; Stouffer, 1940), the push-and-pull framework is the most well-known and most widely used. It was Everett S. Lee who developed it into a model. He argues that both home and host countries have push (minus) and pull (plus) factors and that there are "intervening obstacles" (i.e., factors in between the home and host countries) such as distance, immigration laws, and transportation costs as well as personal factors such as personal sensitivities, intelligence, and awareness of conditions (Lee, 1966, p. 51). Donald Bogue (1969), one of the leading demographers in the United States enriched the model by identifying specific push-and-pull factors. The push factors in his list include decline in a national resource, loss of employment, oppressive or repressive discriminatory treatment, alienation, and retreat from a community because of ideological reasons, lack of opportunities, or catastrophe. The pull factors include superior opportunities for employment, opportunities to earn a larger income or to obtain desired education or training, preferable environment and living conditions, the movement of dependents, or lure of new or different activities, environments, or people.

   Among the early works that used the push-and-pull framework in education, Agarwal and Winkler (1985) identify the following factors as the principal flow drivers: per capita income in the home country, the price or cost of education, the education opportunities available in the home country, and expected benefits of studying abroad. Altbach (1991) identifies as an important push factor the unfavorable conditions in home countries, and pull factors include advanced research facilities, congenial socioeconomic and political environments, and the prospect of multinational classmates. McMahon (1992), after examining the flow of international students from developing to developed countries in the 1960s and 1970s, identifies the following push factors: the level of economic wealth, the degree of involvement of the developing country in the world economy, the priority placed on education by the government of the developing country, and the availability of educational opportunities in the home country. The following pull factors are identified in his study: the relative sizes of the student's home country economy compared to the host country, economic links between the home and host country, host nation political interests in the home country through foreign assistance or cultural links, and host nation support of international students via scholarships or other assistance.

Mazzarol, Kemp, and Savery (1997) identify the following six pull factors: (1) overall level of knowledge and awareness of the host country in the students' home country; (2) level of referrals or personal recommendations that the study destination receives from parents, relatives, friends, and other "gatekeepers" prior to making the final decision; (3) cost issues, including the financial cost of fees, living expenses, travel costs and social costs, such as crime, safety, and racial discrimination; (4) environment, which refers to the study "climate" in the destination country, as well as its physical climate and lifestyle; (5) geographic proximity, which is related to the geographic (and time) proximity of the potential destination country to the students' country; and (6) social links, which is related to whether a student has family or friends living in the destination country and whether family and friends have studied there previously. Mazzarol and Soutar (2002) list "the desire to have a better understanding of the Western culture" as another pull factor. Azmat et al. (2013) expand the Mazzarol and Soutar (2002) study by identifying additional push factors such as economic wealth, educational opportunity, educational standards, and family influence, and additional pull factors such as university reputation, quality and choice of programs, staff quality and permanent residency. A more recent study by Foster (2014) identify four groups of factors, namely, cost, past social relationships, language, and homesickness.

Worth of mentioning is the improved push-and-pull framework proposed by Li and Bray (2007) which is the main framework used in the analysis of this chapter. Li and Bray (2007) call the pull factors in home countries and push factors in host countries "reverse push-pull factors" (p. 795), and they distinguish among four groups of factors: (1) push factors in home countries and (2) pull factors in host countries, both of which provide pushing force for motivating students to leave their home countries, as well as (3) pull factors in home countries, and (4) push factors in host countries, both of which are pulling force for students not to leave their countries. To further develop the push-and-pull factor framework, Li and Bray (2007) proposed to use four categories of motives: academic, economic, social and cultural, and political.

Even though studies have been done on factors affecting Chinese students' decision-making in studying overseas, they are either about reasons why they choose certain countries, such as Australia and the United Kingdom (Azmat et al. 2013; Counsell, 2011; Iannelli & Huang, 2014), or about the mobility of Chinese students within Greater China, including Hong Kong, Macao, and Taiwan (Bodycott & Lai, 2012; Li & Bray, 2007; To, Lung, Lai, & Lai, 2014). Bodycott (2009) is among the few studies examining factors affecting Chinese students' choice of study-abroad destinations using empirical data, and its mixed-method design helped to provide valuable information on Chinese students' motives in studying overseas along with their parents' attitudes. However, the focus of this study is how children and parents differ in their ratings of the factors. Further, the participants in this study were recruited at international education exhibitions or information sessions on studying overseas, which limited the generalizability of the findings as people attending those events were self-selected. Further, the sample size was only 100, which was quite small.

Methods

Research Questions

This study seeks to provide a thorough examination of Chinese students' motives in studying overseas, as well as the relationship between those factors and students' family socioeconomic status. Three research questions are addressed:

1. What are the characteristics of Chinese high school students who plan to study overseas?
2. What factors affect Chinese high school students' decision-making in going abroad to study?

Data Collection

The data used in this study were collected at six public high schools in each of the three cities of Beijing, Shenzhen, and Chengdu, making it a total of 18 schools. Altogether 3275 surveys were distributed at those schools, and 3001 of them were completed and returned, which resulted in a high response rate of 91.6%, thanks to the assistance of the schools in distributing and collecting the survey. The survey included information on students' demographics, socioeconomic status, plans regarding studying overseas, reasons for and concerns over studying overseas, perceived costs and benefits of studying overseas.

The three cities of Beijing, Shenzhen, and Chengdu were chosen to represent large cities in China since those cities are where the majority of Chinese students studying overseas come from. Beijing is located in the Northern part of China, and as the nation's capital, it is a political and cultural center. Shenzhen is located in the Southern part and along the coastal line, and as the first and largest Special Economic Zone in South China, it is among the most economically advanced cities in China. Chengdu is located in the Southwest, and as the capital of Sichuan Province which is the largest province in China, it is the cultural and economic center in the Western region of China.

This study makes contributions to the existing body of literature on the motives and decision-making process of Chinese students in the following three aspects. First, the use of large-scale dataset from three cities located in different parts of China provide a better representation of the student population and thus enable the researchers to do a more comprehensive investigation on the motives and decision-making among Chinese high school students. Second, although there have been studies done on the factors related to international student mobility and also Chinese students' flow out of China, they are mostly at the postsecondary level. This empirical study is among the first to examine Chinese students at the high school level. Unlike other studies which gather information from students who are already enrolled in a postsecondary institution overseas, this study investigates their motives and decision-making process while they are still in the preparation or decision-making stage. Third, this study is the first to examine how the factors are related to students' family SES, and knowing more about this relationship may have important implications for preparations that need to be done on the students' part, as well as improvement that could be made in the recruitment and service efforts on schools' part.

Findings and Discussion

Characteristics of Participants: Those Who Plan to Study Overseas Vs. Those Who Do Not

Individual Characteristics

Among the 2927 participants, 26.0% specifically state that they do not have the plan to study overseas, and 27.9% are undecided. About 44.3% state that they plan to study overseas, which is a considerable proportion, and it includes 2.4% who plan to attend high school overseas, 24.1% who plan to do undergraduate study overseas, and 17.8% who plan to do graduate study overseas. As shown in Table 4.1, 55.7% of the participants ($N = 2978$) are female, and the average age of the participants is 17.4 ($N = 2854$).

Generally speaking, students planning to study overseas have better academic performance than those not planning to study overseas and those who are undecided. For example, 23.5% of the students planning to study overseas rank themselves among the top 10% ($N = 1122$) in their overall academic performance, as compared to 12.9% for students not planning to study overseas ($N = 703$), and 11.8% for undecided students ($N = 740$). The differences among those three groups of students in their overall academic performance is statistically significant ($p < 0.001$). Among the three main subjects of math, English and Chinese, the differences among the three groups seem to be the largest for English ($p < 0.001$).

Family Characteristics

Accompanying the rapid economic development and the establishment of market as the dominating force for allocating resources, China has been undergoing social transformation which is characterized by rapid social stratification during the past several decades. According to Lu Xueyi, a renowned sociologist in China, the largest change in social strata in recent years lies in the increase in the number of white-collar workers and professionals, civil servants, and private business owners, which all belong to the rising "middle class" (Lu, 2010). In particular, two social groups have caught attention in recent years among the public, the media, as well as

Table 4.1 Summary statistics, overall, and by plan for studying overseas

Demographic	Overall	Students planning to study overseas	Students not planning to study overseas	Undecided students
*Female**	55.9 ($N = 2978$)	58.6 ($N = 784$)	50.2 ($N = 380$)	56.8 ($N = 459$)
Age[a]	17.4 (0.02) $N = 2854$	17.3 (0.03) $N = 1284$	17.5 (0.04) $N = 729$	17.3 (0.04) $N = 774$
Academic performance (at school)				
Overall**	$N - 2620$	$N = 1122$	$N = 703$	$N = 740$
Top 10%	17.1	23.5	12.9	11.8
11–30%	30.2	29.4	30.4	30.9
31–50%	26.3	26.3	24.6	28.1
Below 50%	26.5	20.8	32.0	29.2
*Math***	$N = 2512$	$N = 1079$	$N = 677$	$N = 708$
Top 10%	17.5	23.8	15.2	10.3
11–30%	29.9	30.3	27.2	31.6
31–50%	26.9	25.0	27.6	29.2
Below 50%	25.6	20.9	30.0	28.8
*English***	$N = 2516$	$N = 1077$	$N = 676$	$N = 713$
Top 10%	19.0	27.2	12.0	13.6
11–30%	27.2	29.1	25.1	25.9
31–50%	25.3	22.4	24.3	30.9
Below 50%	28.5	21.4	38.6	29.6
*Chinese***	$N = 2503$	$N = 1069$	$N = 676$	$N = 710$
Top 10%	18.0	25.4	13.0	11.5
11–30%	30.2	28.8	31.8	31.0
31–50%	27.6	24.8	29.0	31.0
Below 50%	24.1	21.0	26.2	26.5
*Father's education***	$N = 2822$	$N = 1270$	$N = 728$	$N = 764$
Associate or below	50.4	33.9	64.7	64.3
Bachelor's degree	33.5	40.9	26.2	28.4
Graduate degree	16.1	25.2	9.1	7.3
*Mother's education***	$N = 2812$	$N = 1266$	$N = 723$	$N = 763$
Associate or below	57.8	42.3	71.4	70.9
Bachelor's degree	31.3	41.1	22.0	24.0
Graduate degree	10.9	16.6	6.6	5.1
*Father's occupation***	$N = 2777$	$N = 1246$	$N = 719$	$N = 760$
Government official	8.3	10.8	6.7	5.9
Business	40.9	46.1	33.7	40.0
Professional	18.1	18.9	18.6	16.3

(continued)

Table 4.1 (continued)

Demographic	Overall	Students planning to study overseas	Students not planning to study overseas	Undecided students
Worker, farmer, and other	32.7	24.2	41.0	37.8
*Family annual income (2014)***	N = 1172	N = 481	N = 369	N = 298
<100,000 yuan	30.4	15.8	42.0	39.3
100,000–190,000 yuan	28.7	22.7	33.1	33.6
200,000–290,000 yuan	13.0	16.2	10.6	11.1
300,000–490,000 yuan	9.7	15.2	4.6	7.4
500,000–1 million yuan	9.4	15.0	5.1	6.0
>1 million yuan	8.8	15.2	4.6	2.7

[a]Means are shown, and standard deviations are in parenthesis. Percentages are reported for the rest of the variables. Test results are from Chi-square tests
*$p < 0.1$
**$p < 0.001$

scholars and researchers, and they are labeled "*fuerdai*" and "*guanerdai*," which refer to the offspring of government officials and wealthy business people, respectively. Showered with inherited privilege of power and wealth, those children carry important labels of new social strata (Zhang, 2013).

The following analysis on family characteristics and on the relationship between family SES and motivating factors pays particular attention to those groups which are at an advantage in building networks and mobilizing social resources, namely, civil servants (referred to as "Official" hereafter), business owners ("Business" hereafter), and white-collar professionals ("Professional" hereafter). Children of those three groups are examined in reference to others ("Other" hereafter) in order to have a more nuanced understanding of how family SES is related to students' motives in studying overseas as those three subgroups of students are likely to enjoy more social resources because of their advantaged social status.

Overall, the parental educational level of the participants seems to be pretty high compared to the general population: 33.5% of the students have a father with a bachelor's degree and 16.1% a graduate degree ($N = 2822$); 31.3% of the mother with a bachelor's degree and 30.9 a graduate degree ($N = 2812$). Since there is a well-established high correlation between parental education and parental occupation, it is no surprise that the occupation of the participating students seem to be of relatively high social status: 8.3% of the fathers are government officials, 40.9% are business people, 18.1% are professionals, and only 32.7% belong to other relatively disadvantaged social strata ($N = 2777$). Family annual income also seems to indicate that the participating students tend to come from relatively privileged family backgrounds: Among the participants who provided valid information, only 30.4% of the family had an annual family income below 100,000 yuan[1] in 2014, 69.6% of the family had an annual income above 100,000 yuan, including 8.8% above one million yuan. The relatively privileged family backgrounds of the participants reflect the relatively high family socioeconomic status of residents in large cities, which has the highest concentration of high-income population with high educational level and high professional status. By comparison, students planning to study overseas have more privileged family backgrounds than those who do not plan to study overseas and those who are undecided, as reflected in higher parental educational level, parental occupation with higher social status, and high family income.

To sum up, students who plan to study overseas distinguish themselves from the other students by relatively high academic performance and high family socioeconomic status indicated by parental education, parental profession, and family income. In other words, it seems that, in order for students to have the determination to study overseas, they need to have confidence in both their own academic capability and their family's financial capability to support them. Interestingly, there is no evidence suggesting any differentials among the three cities in the characteristics of students who plan to study overseas and their family backgrounds.

Factors Affecting Students' Decision-Making

Table 4.2 presents the top three factors affecting students' decision-making in studying overseas. Those factors are categorized in Fig. 4.1 using the framework proposed in Li and Bray (2007).

Academic Factors

As shown in Table 4.2, among the 1384 students who plan to go overseas to study, the top three education-related reasons for studying overseas are (1) the inferior overall quality of domestic institutions, (2) intense competition, and (3) lack of the programs of my interest. Academically, educational quality and educational opportunity seem to be the biggest factors. This finding confirms existing studies which proved dissatisfaction of Chinese students and their families with the increasingly crowded environment of the higher education system in China, as well as with the quality of curricula and teaching methods "which are considered to be not as advanced and up-to-date as those adopted by higher education institutions in Western countries" (Iannelli & Huang, 2014, p. 808).

In spite of the rapid expansion of Chinese higher education during the past few decades, it is still quite competitive to enter a decent college or university. In 2015,

---

[1] In 2014, the exchange rate between US dollar and yuan was about 6.2.

Table 4.2 Factors related to students' decision-making in studying overseas

Factors	No. 1	No. 2	No. 3
Education-related reasons for studying overseas ($N = 1384$)	Inferior overall quality of domestic institutions (48.5[a])	Intense competition (15.0)	Lack of programs of my interest (12.8)
Reasons for choosing an institution ($N = 1354$)	High-quality teaching staff (29.7)	Good reputation (29.0)	Innovation in teaching and research (17.7)
Reasons for choosing a country ($N = 1277$)	High-quality education (46.4)	Advanced science and technology (14.0)	Diverse culture (11.4)
Destination country of choice ($N = 1275$)	The United States (61.6)	The United Kingdom (11.5)	Canada (7.6)
Non-educational reasons for studying overseas ($N = 1340$)	Gaining global perspectives (32.7)	Better career prospect (17.5)	Experiencing another culture (14.8)
Concerns over studying overseas ($N = 2635$)	High cost (37.0)	Language barrier (19.1)	Away from family and friends (10.4)
Benefits of studying overseas ($N = 1156$)	Learning advanced technology (34.2)	Gaining global perspective (17.8)	Obtaining a foreign diploma which carries more weight (13.0)

[a]Percentages are reported in parenthesis

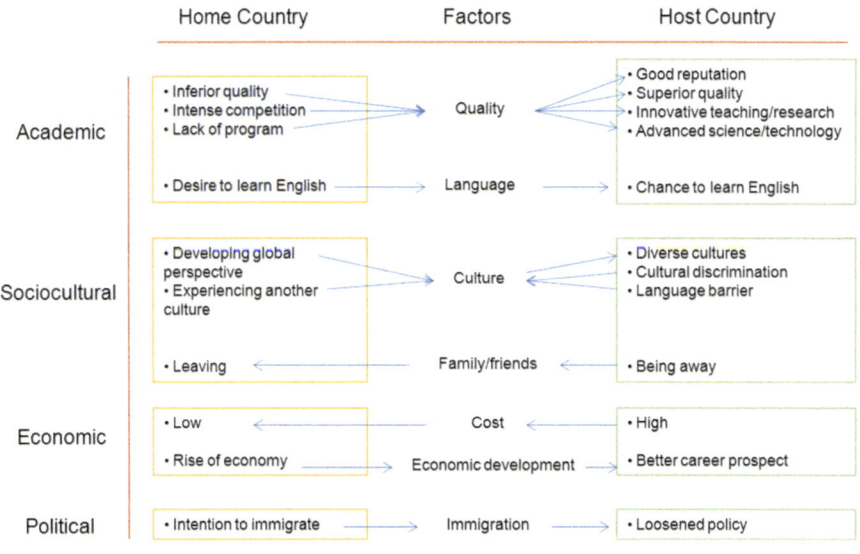

Fig. 4.1 Summary of push-and-pull factors

the total enrollment at higher education institutions was nearly 36.47 million (Ministry of Education, 2016), and the enrollment rate among students between the ages of 18 and 22 reached 40.0%, compared to 15% in 2002 and 3.4% in 1990 (Wu & Lu, 2002). Nonetheless, the National College-Entrance Examination is still the main avenue through which students can access higher education. As a result, the competition for entering a quality higher education institution is still quite intense.

Corresponding to the above-mentioned factors in China which are pushing Chinese students overseas are better university reputation as well as high quality and more choice of programs in host countries which serve as pulling forces. In evaluating an institution's quality, 29.7% of the participants rank "high-quality teaching staff" as the No. 1 factor, 29.0% rank "good reputation" as the No. 2 factor, and 17.7% rank "innovation in teaching and research" as the No. 3 factor ($N = 1354$). The importance of academic reasons for studying overseas is highlighted by the fact that "learning advanced technology" is ranked as the No. 1 perceived benefit of studying overseas. Those academic pulling forces in host countries are confirmed by existing literature (Azmat et al., 2013; Iannelli & Huang, 2014; To et al., 2014).

In other words, the major motive behind the Chinese student mobility seems to be learning, which is rather reassuring, especially considering recent media coverage on international students from China who do nothing but showing off their wealth. As a recent report in *the Chronicle of Higher Education* says: "Here's what Americans think about the Chinese students who have been crowding their campuses: They all drive fancy cars, and they all are rich" (Fischer, 2015).[2] The Chinese students who go overseas in recent years are very different from their predecessors who had embarked on the same journey two decades earlier. A recent article in *Foreign Policy* (Liu, 2015) depicts some typical Chinese students studying overseas in the 1980s and 1990s: They tended to be among "the nation's best and brightest"; they are usually "… penniless … didn't go out to dinner, didn't go to parties, and assumed that American students were all really rich"; and they tended to be "idealistic and patriotic." In less than two decades, the image of the humble and diligent Chinese students studying overseas has transformed drastically and is replaced by the image of the "nouveau riche," or "the second-generation scion in a wealthy family, who studies abroad in order to return home to run the family business." They "pay full tuition, often study finance, business management, or economics, and spend their time clustered together"; and they drive luxury cars and go into the city "for extravagant weekend shopping trips." As Liu pithily summarized: "It's not just a thickening wallet that separates yesterday's overseas Chinese student from today's. Many have noted a shift in the academic goals and underlying motivations pulling Chinese scholars" to study overseas.

In spite of the negative media coverage, it seems that learning is still the main driving force behind the large outflow of Chinese students, and the importance of learning is confirmed by the reasons for students' top three choices of No. 1

---

[2] For more reports on Chinese students showing off their wealth, please refer to Higgins (2013) on Bloomberg and Drash (2015) on CNN.

destination country, which are the United States, the United Kingdom, and Canada. 46.4% of the participants choose "high-quality education" as the No. 1 reason ($N = 1277$).

Sociocultural Factors

As Beine, Noel, and Ragot (2013) indicated, cross-border migration of international students may also be viewed as a consumption choice. In that case, students not only consider the returns to their educational investment, they also consider the circumstances and the place where they will study. The facts that "gaining global perspectives" is ranked as the No. 1 non-educational reason for studying overseas, and that "diverse culture" is ranked the No. 3 reason for choosing a particular country, all demonstrate that social and cultural experiences are important considerations for Chinese students in their decision-making regarding studying overseas. In fact, 22.1% of the participants ($N = 1101$) indicate that they do not care whether they will be able to recover the cost of studying overseas.

A few in-depth stories in a recent report in *the Chronicle of Higher Education* depicting Chinese families who send their children overseas reflect the importance of sociocultural factors in the decision-making process (Fischer, 2015). Abby Wu has a mother who is an executive in a prosperous Chinese company and father who works in satellite communication. In spite of their high-paying jobs, Abby's parents describe themselves as a "normal family," which means that they lack the "connections" which can help one "secure a position, particularly in government or state-owned companies." Her parents had contemplated on the option of studying abroad which they thought would guarantee her a "more certain future" since she was in middle school. Beini Wang's parents are both instructors in a local university, and they had dreamed about sending their daughter overseas to study because they wanted her to "learn something" and they thought the test-centric educational system in China was "exhausting and boring." Being professionals whose combined yearly salaries of 200,000 yuan (an equivalent of $32,000), paying for an American undergraduate education is out of the question. But they sold their large, well-located apartment and bought a smaller, less expensive one, which helped them to pay for the cost. It is not uncommon for families to pay for an education abroad using the profit made from the skyrocketing real-estate prices. Like most Chinese parents, Beini's parents think it is well worth it. "It's not an investment," her mother says, "It's our child's life." As the report summarizes: "For Chinese parents, the choice of an American education for their child—and almost always their only child—is not just a financial investment. It's a political maneuver, a personal sacrifice, a bet on greater opportunity abroad."

As counter force to the above-mentioned external sociocultural pull factors, external sociocultural push factors such as cultural and language barriers, as well as having to be away from family and friends, serve to deter students. As a culture that attaches great importance to family and values friendship, it is conceivable that

Chinese students may not want to go overseas to study because they do not want to be away from their family and friends.

Economic Factors

From a human capital perspective, going to another country to study is considered an investment and the motive is to have better job opportunities and thus higher expected income in the future. In fact, 17.5% of the participants rated "better career prospects" as the No. 2 non-educational reason for studying overseas. Therefore, those economic considerations serve as important pulling forces in destination countries. And along with them, the rise of China's economy serves as an important pushing force within China. Studying overseas used to be the privilege reserved for the few most wealthy and powerful elite in China, but now even an average white-collar professional can afford to send their children abroad thanks to the rapid economic development in China, which is reflected in higher living standards, more wealth accumulated among individuals, skyrocketing real-estate price, as well as the appreciation of the Chinese currency.

In spite of the increasing affordability of studying overseas, its financial cost is still a major consideration for most Chinese families, and thus serves as a push factor in host countries. As shown in Table 4.2, 37.0% of the participants identify "high cost" as the No. 1 concern, and 17.5% of those who plan to study overseas rank "better career aspect" (which is associated with higher income) as the No. 2 non-educational reason. Further, 52.8% of the participants think that they would consider studying overseas only if the cost accounts for less than 30% of their annual family income, 21.9% can accept between 30 and 50%, and only 10.5% can accept above 50% ($N = 2634$). In addition, 56.5% of the participants expect to recover the cost of studying overseas within 5 years after graduation, 16.6% between 5 and 10 years and 2.1% between 10 and 15 years ($N = 1101$).

Political Factors

Loosened restrictions on visa and immigration in host countries have been identified as a pulling force (Bodycott, 2009; Lee, 1966; To et al., 2014). Interestingly, this does not prove to be an important factor among Chinese students. For example, only 6.7% of the participants ($N = 1340$) who plan to study overseas identify immigration as the No. 1 non-educational reason for studying overseas, and only 2.3% ($N = 1277$) of them choose loosened immigration policy as the No. 1 reason for choosing a particular country.

Conclusions

As the world becomes increasingly interconnected and interdependent economically, politically, culturally, and socially, international student mobility can only become more frequent and thus remains an important topic. Using the push-and-pull framework based on data collected from 3001 students at 18 high schools located in the three cities of Beijing, Shenzhen, and Chengdu, this study identifies important factors in the academic, economic, sociocultural, and political aspects that serve as the pushing and pulling forces in students' decision-making process of studying overseas. The finding that sociocultural factors such as "experiencing another culture" and "gaining global perspective" play a significant role is an interesting one. Further, the findings reveal the importance of students' academic preparation and their families' financial capability.

Currently, the majority of Chinese students studying overseas come from large cities, and the choice of the three cities of Beijing, Shenzhen, and Chengdu in this study was made to reflect this trend. However, sporadic data has shown that this trend has been trickling down to smaller cities. Worth mentioning is that studies conducted by the authors in a small city on the east coast of China have shown similar trends in terms of students' motives in and families' decision-making about studying overseas.

References

Agarwal, V. B., & Winkler, D. R. (1985). Migration of foreign students to the United States. *The Journal of Higher Education, 56*(5), 509–522.

Altbach, P. G. (1991). Impact and adjustment: Foreign students in comparative perspective. *Higher Education, 21*(3), 305–323.

Altbach, P. G., & Knight, J. (2007). The internationalization of higher education: Motivations and realities. *Journal of Studies in International Education, 11*(3/4), 290–305.

Azmat, F., Osborne, A., Rossignol, K. L., Jogulu, U., Rentschler, R., Robottom, I., et al. (2013). Understanding aspirations and expectations of international students in Australian higher education. *Asia Pacific Journal of Education, 33*(1), 97–111.

Bartlett, T., & Fischer, K. (2011, November 3). The China conundrum: American colleges find the Chinese student boon a tricky fit. *The Chronicle of Higher Education*.

Beine, M., Noel R., & Ragot, L. (2013). *The determinants of international mobility of students*. CEPII working paper.

Bodycott, P. (2009). Choosing a higher education study abroad destination: What mainland Chinese parents and students rate as important. *Journal of Research in International Education, 8*(3), 349–373.

Bodycott, P., & Lai, A. (2012). The influence and implications of Chinese culture in the decision to undertake cross-border higher education. *Journal of Studies in International Education, 16*(3), 252–270.

Bogue, D. J. (1969). *Principles of demography*. New York, NY: John Wiley & Sons.

Counsell, D. (2011). Chinese students abroad: Why they choose the UK and how they see their future. *China: An International Journal, 9*(1), 48–71.

Drash, W. (2015, August 5). *Culture clash in Iowa: The town where bubble tea shops outnumber Starbucks*. CNN

Fischer, K. (2015, July 6). The Chinese mother's American dream. *The Chronicle of Higher Education*.

Foster, M. (2014). Student destination choices in higher education: Exploring attitudes of Brazilian students to study in the United Kingdom. *Journal of Research in International Education, 13*(2), 149–162.

Higgins, T. (2013, December 19). Chinese students major in luxury cars. Bloomberg.

Iannelli, C., & Huang, J. (2014). Trends in participation and attainment of Chinese students in UK higher education. *Studies in Higher Education, 39*(5), 805–855.

IIE. (2016). *Open Doors*. Washington, DC: Institute of International Education.

Johnson, V. (2003). The perils of homeland security: When we hinder foreign students and scholars, we endanger our national security. *The Chronicle of Higher Education, 49*(31), B7.

Kinnell, M. (1989). International marketing in UK higher education: Some issues in relation to marketing educational programmes to overseas students. *European Journal of Marketing, 23*(5), 7–21.

Knight, J. (2011). Education hubs: A fad, a brand, an innovation? *Journal of Studies in International Education, 15*(3), 221–240.

Lee, E. S. (1966). A theory of migration. *Demography, 3*(1), 47–57.

Li, M., & Bray, M. (2007). Cross-border flows of students for higher education: Push-pull factors and motivations of mainland Chinese students in Hong Kong and Macau. *Higher Education, 53*, 791–818.

Li, W., & Zhang, Y. (2011, November 3). Sharp tuition increase makes it increasingly expensive to study in UK and US. *People's Daily*.

Liu, Y. (2015, September 1). China's nouveau rich have landed on America's campuses. Foreign Policy Retrieved March 26, 2016, from http://foreignpolicy.com/2015/09/01/chinas-nouveau-riche-have-landed-on-americas-campuses/

Lu, X. (2010). *Social structure in contemporary China*. Beijing: Social Sciences Academic Press.

Marginson, S. (2011). It's a long way down: The underlying tension in the education export industry. *Australian Universities' Review, 53*(2), 21–33.

Mazzarol, T., Kemp, S., & Savery, L. (1997). *International students who choose not to study in Australia: An examination of Taiwan and Indonesia*. Canberra: Australian Education Foundation.

Mazzarol, T., & Soutar, G. N. (2002). "Push-pull" factors influencing international student destination choice. *International Journal of Educational Management, 16*(2), 82–90.

McMahon, M. E. (1992). Higher education in a world market: A historical look at the global context of international study. *Higher Education, 24*(4), 465–482.

Ministry of Education. (2016). Education Communique 2015. Retrieved September 8, 2016, from http://moe.edu.cn/srcsite/A03/s180/moe_633/201607/t20160706_270976.html

OECD. (2014). *Education at a glance*. Paris: Organization for Economic Co-operation and Development.

OECD. (2015). *Education at a glance*. Paris: Organization for Economic Co-operation and Development.

Perkins, R., & Neumayer, E. (2014). Geographies of educational mobilities: Exploring the uneven flows of international students. *The Geographical Journal, 180*(3), 246–259.

Ravenstein, E. G. (1885). The laws of migration. *Journal of the Royal Statistical Society, 48*(part 2), 167–227.

Rogers, K. (1984). Foreign students: Economic benefit or liability: Practical advice for colleges or universities that want to attract foreign students. *The College Board Review, 133*, 20–25.

Stouffer, S. A. (1940). Intervening opportunities and competing migration. *Journal of Regional Science, 2*, 1–26.

Tan, J. (2013). Introduction. In *The international mobility of students in Asia and the Pacific*. Bangkok: UNESCO.

Throsby, C. D. (1986). Economic aspect of the foreign student question. *The Economic Record, 62*(4), 400–414.

To, W. M., Lung, J. W. Y., Lai, L. S. L., & Lai, T. M. (2014). Destination choice of cross-border Chinese students: An importance-performance analysis. *Educational Studies, 40*(1), 63–80.

Wu, X., & Lu, Y. (2002). The pressure faced by higher education institutions against their expansion and some policy discussion. *Guangxi Higher Education Research, 1*, 39–41.

Zhang, J. (2013). *Fuerdai* and *Guanerdai*: Commonalities and differences in the structure of media language. *Modern Communications, 3*, 49–54.

Chapter 5
The Push–Pull Framework and the Decision-Making Process of Chinese Students

Introduction

This chapter advances the task of the previous chapter and enriches the push–pull framework (hereafter the framework) in international student mobility studies.[1] Drawing on in-depth interviews with three Chinese students in the United States,[1] this chapter substantiates the relevance and utility of this framework in understanding Chinese students' motivations and decision-making process regarding overseas studies. Their stories corroborate multiple patterns revealed in the previous chapter and other existing studies of this framework. For example, although the three students came from different regions of China and are in different programs in the United States, the major gravitational pull of the United States—in accordance with previous findings—is the academic prestige of the US higher education system. The fact that two of them consider the intense competition of the Chinese education system and corporate environment also echoes the findings of previous research (e.g., Li & Bray, 2007; Park, 2009; Tan, 2013). My findings on the significance of students' social networks also support the conclusion of some existing studies on international students in non-US countries, such as Turkey (Kondakci, 2011).

Furthermore, these students' nuanced stories are drawn upon to highlight how to further develop the framework. One area of improvement lies in existing studies's tendency to conceptualize particular push or pull factors statically. As will be shown, decision-making for overseas studies is a fluid process in which students and their parents constantly reframe the same pull or push factor in different directions.[2] In

---

[1] I selected these three students based on the richness of their stories, rather than their generalizability to the overall pattern of Chinese overseas students. With that said, I managed to select one undergraduate student, one PhD student and one professional student to broaden the comprehensiveness of the inquiry.

[2] According to Findlay, Prazeres, McCollum, and Packwood (2017), there is "fluidity in life plans." I have also suggested previously that decision-making for overseas studies is not necessarily

© Springer Nature Singapore Pte Ltd. 2020
B. Cheng et al., *The New Journey to the West*, Education in the Asia-Pacific
Region: Issues, Concerns and Prospects 53,
https://doi.org/10.1007/978-981-15-5588-6_5

some cases, decision-makers can go so far as to translate a factor that has been pre-viously conceived as a push factor into a pull. For example, one of my informants initially considered the pizza-dominated food culture in the United States a "push from host countries," but she later translated it into a "pull from host countries" when she was prepared to challenge herself in her life skills and adaptability to new environments.

Another area of reflection concerns the mechanisms through which students and their parents engage with push and pull factors to make decisions about overseas stud-ies. The premise in the extant literature is that individual decision-makers engage *directly* with various factors at the nation-state level as push and pull forces. However, the stories in this chapter showcase a variety of intermediaries (e.g., test-preparation schools, educational consulting firms and alumni networks) that interpret push–pull factors for decision-makers.[3] The details of informants' stories show how these inter-mediaries can frame a factor that has been commonly perceived as a push of the host country into a pull. At the end of the chapter, these areas of improvement are revisited and the implications of the findings for the push–pull framework are discussed.

Yan: The Influence of Family and the Competition in Chinese Education System

Yan (pseudonym) is a second-year undergraduate student at a state university in the United States. She is from a major city in Western China and plans to major in den-tal hygiene. When discussing her motivation for studying in the United States, she highlights the US academic environment as the pull factor, and a series of other factors that have pushed her out of China.

Yan's parents are professors in a Chinese university. Under their influence, Yan has long admired the learning and academic environment of the United States:

> *My mom talks about US universities every day. She said, "Harvard University's library has its lights on until 4 a.m. All students there work hard. They study hard with good self-discipline." So it sounds like a great learning environment. I found the idea of self-discipline appealing. You know, I found myself sometimes disciplined, but sometimes not. So I figured it would be a great opportunity to further improve myself (by studying abroad—the author add the words in this and other parentheses to clarify quotes by informants). I wanted to find out if I can adapt to the learning environment here, and if I can follow every step.*

Her accounts reveal her mother's role in shaping her admiration for the US aca-demic environment. In addition, her family's embeddedness in, and her previous experience with, the Chinese education system induced her to consider this system a force pushing her out of China. She describes how she developed the desire to escape China's education system:

---

premeditated with clear goals or with costs and benefits thoroughly weighted (Lin 2020). As a fluid process, the decision on overseas studies can emerge in an incremental and experimental fashion.

[3] I do not categorize parents as intermediaries because they often act as decision-makers, especially for young students. Having said that, the rest of this chapter will illustrate how parents, along with other intermediaries, interpret push and pull factors for students.

> *My parents are professors in China. So I know very well how they teach, and I have seen how Chinese college students live their lives ever since my childhood. I have no interest in that kind of life. There are all kinds of control there. You know, all the students there live in dorms, and those old ladies supervising dorms are tough, keeping all the students in the dorms. But students still run out of the dorm (for entertainment) all the time. So those regulations do not really matter. They are all symbolic. Also, every class in Chinese universities has a director. My father used to be a director. He is a responsible one. But a lot of other people are not. So it is really up to the specific person. You know, a lot of things in China are about relationships and connections. It is not about following rules. I don't like that.*

Yan's disdain for Chinese universities is one of the engines that prompted her to opt for overseas studies. Her story below corroborates Iannelli and Huang's (2014) findings with regard to competitive pressure being a common push factor of the home country. Further conversations reveal a long process through which her tolerance for the Chinese education system diminished. She mentioned the mounting competitive pressure in her first of high school year as a novel push factor she had not experienced in middle school. She traces how the idea to study abroad developed:

> *My mom asked me during my middle-school years about whether I would like to study abroad. I felt that she was ready then. But I was not. I told her, "Students in the U.S. are bad at math but my friends here are good". You know, I was interested in math at that time. I did pretty well on math exams. I was thinking about staying in China. I said "no". Then, I had this huge regret after I started high school. "Why didn't I leave?" There was just too much pressure. I wanted to learn math well, but I just couldn't. I was really longing for a life that was easier. I was getting more and more into studying abroad.*

Other push–pull factors outlined in the previous chapter, such as the pull from the home country and the push from the host country, also influenced Yan's decision. For example, she mentioned the familiar environment and easy lifestyle in Chinese colleges as pull factors from the home country. These factors indeed induced her to think twice when she was making decisions about overseas studies. However, since she had prioritized academic prestige over other factors, she was able to translate the potential lifestyle challenges in the United States into a pull from the host country:

> *You know, I was worried whether I could take care of myself after coming here. College life in China is easy. When you receive the offer letter, you also receive a debit card. Your life is being taken care of. But later, I convinced myself to come here. I mean I could polish my life skills when I left China. I did not want to attend a Chinese college anyway.*

This suggests the fluidity in engaging the push–pull factors in the decision-making process. When a student has prioritized one factor (e.g., the academic prestige of the host country), he or she can translate another push or pull factor into a different category. Moreover, the same push or pull factor is subject to reconsideration and re-interpretation by the same student over time. It is not uncommon for a student, such as Yan, to consider lifestyle difficulty a push from the host country one day, but to reassess it as a pull from the host country later.

While some studies find that students decide why and where to study in separate steps (e.g., Mazzarol and Soutar, 2002; Park, 2009), my findings suggest that these two questions are often inseparable when students are making decisions. In Yan's case, her familiarity with the United States and admiration for its academic prestige facilitated her decision to study abroad. She elaborates on her choice to study in the United States:

> *I have been most interested in the US ever since I was a child. My mom did her PhD here (at the same university as mine) and she brought me here once. Once when she was attending a class, I observed in the classroom. So I could feel that it was different here…. There were also four or five senior students at my high school in China. They later attended high schools in the US and went to good US colleges. So I was getting a bit red-eyed (jealous).*

It is evident that her choice of the United States as her destination has not been based directly on the academic prestige of US higher education. Rather, her family members, alumni networks, and even her prior experience in the United States, had also influenced her confidence in the US higher education.

Ailing: **The Role of Social Network in Framing Push and Pull**

Ailing is a first-year PhD student in mechanical engineering at a state university in the United States. Born in 1983, she had already received her master's degree in China before overseas studies. Interested in exposing herself to Western science and technology, and influenced by her overseas alumni networks, Ailing never doubted that she would study abroad one day. However, as will be shown, the language barrier and English-based standardized tests made her reconsider her location of choice. Her case reminds us of the role of social networks in students' decision-making process. It also introduces the often-overlooked test-preparation and application processes as push-pull factors. Ailing elaborates on the genesis behind her motivation for overseas studies and the role of overseas alumni networks:

> *That was my second year in the master's program (in China). Students of senior cohorts in our lab were applying for different programs in Europe and the US. There were also senior students who had already lived overseas. They came back and talked to us about their lives overseas. So the things they talked about made me feel good. I mean I saw that they had broader visions. So I got this plan (for overseas studies) already…. They (students of senior cohorts) were the major source of information for us. You know, each year about half of the student body in our lab goes abroad…. This includes both the master's and PhD students. From their experience, I felt that we could get in touch with different perspectives and directions (by studying abroad). You know, for science and technology programs, you want to get in touch with these different perspectives. You want to have an inter-disciplinary perspective to publish good articles. That's why I changed from chemistry to mechanical engineering after I left China. That way I could combine the knowledge I had already learned.*

The quotation above reveals the perceived academic advantages of the United States and Europe in terms of interdisciplinary research and broad vision. These constitute pulls from host countries for Ailing. What is also crucial here is that her alumni network, both domestic and foreign, plays an integral role in framing these academic advantages into the pulls of host countries. When asked whether she had adopted the idea of overseas studies prior to talking with students of senior cohorts, Ailing confirmed their influence.

No, I had not. My original plan was to do both a master's and a PhD program with my advisor (in China). I only started thinking and planning about coming out (of China) after hearing from them (students of senior cohorts).

Similar to the previous case, Ailing had heard that everyday life in Western countries, such as what to eat, was a challenge for overseas Chinese students. She describes the food issue she has encountered in the United States:

There is a friend of mine who came to the US a few years ago. And he went to a state university in Utah. He told me a lot about his lifestyle in the US. I mean he basically talked about everything like food, housing, clothing and transportation, etc. I asked him if he had gotten used to the food here. So he told me he was fine. He only had issues during the first six months. After that, he had had no problem blending in. Actually I had more problems when I had just arrived. The day I arrived was a Saturday and all the cafeterias on campus were closed over the weekend. I was starving for the first two days! I only had instant noodles I had brought with me. The first real food I had was when my advisor treated me to a buffet. But I couldn't eat anything. Everything was so oily! You know, pizza and that kind of stuff. I actually lost weight after I came.

Her account reveals that the lifestyle in the United States can be a push factor of the host country. However, the information she obtained from her friend helped her realize that such an issue was bearable. This example substantiates the earlier point about the role of alumni and friend networks in framing push and pull factors.

Another factor Ailing mentioned was the liability of preparing for English-based standardized tests. The need to prepare for these tests not only affects the decision about whether to study abroad; it also influences students' decisions about where to study. For many Chinese students, these two decisions are inseparable because learning English and preparing for standardized tests such as TOEFL and GRE are not only time-consuming but also challenging, especially for STEM students. Whether a host country requires these tests, which tests and what scores are required, therefore, are issues a student has to consider. In the following account, Ailing explains how the test requirements and her chemistry background led her to choose where to study:

Actually for us STEM students, we don't have to take TOEFL or IELTS if we are going to the UK instead of the US. For many European countries, we only need the interviewer to provide a certificate about our language capacity. Then we can go there directly.... Also, most of my fellow students of senior cohorts went to Europe. People did not want to spend time learning English or preparing for the tests. You know, we were quite busy as master's students (in China) because as chemistry students we worked on a schedule from 8am-11pm, six days a week. So we really did not have much time to prepare for English tests. Very often we only had one day off a week, and sometimes only half a day.

In addition to the countries' varying language test requirements, the disparate program lengths also affected the decision of where to choose for overseas studies. Ailing explains,

Another thing is that it only takes about three years to get a PhD degree in Europe. Germany is an exception. You need four years there. Here in the US you need at least four years. In those higher-ranking universities, it is fairly common for you to spend five years or more (on your PhD). Also, you need to take classes in the US. There is no need for that in Europe. You start working in the lab once you arrive there. You know, taking classes might affect the progress of your lab work.

Indeed, challenging lifestyles, stringent language test requirements, and lengthy programs can become push factors of the host country. To Ailing, these factors render the United States less appealing than staying in China or studying abroad in Europe. However, students tend to translate these pushes into pull factors after they prioritize other determinants, such as academic fitness. Ailing had already been leaning toward the United States since she had discovered that "for STEM students, studying abroad was more about choosing the right advisor than choosing the right country, and I found there was a perfect match between what my current advisor does and what I am interested in." As academic fitness nudged her toward the United States, she started translating the pushes of the United States into pulls:

Of course it was time-consuming to prepare for those language tests. But I figured that preparing for these tests was not a big thing. I still wanted to improve my English (through these tests). I also took those tests so I wouldn't limit myself to European universities. I even went to a local test-preparation school to prepare for the tests.

In addition to translating push and pull factors into different directions, decision-makers sometimes change their stance toward a push or pull factor over time. This is because decision-making is a process rather than a one-time event. New factors, such as abrupt changes in the host country's political environment, can influence the decision-making process. In Ailing's case, she started to think twice about studying in the United States after she had already decided it would be her destination. One of her concerns was recent visa complications associated with the Trump Administration's anti-immigration policies. Ailing explains the impact of these policies on her visa and decisions:

Of course these policies have a huge impact on our visas. My previous program (chemistry) is considered "sensitive"(to national security) and they (the US government) issued a "check" on my visa. In such a case, the validity period for my visa status is shortened. Now I only get a one year visa. Some students of senior cohorts who came here for postdoctoral studies got visas that were only valid for two months! Plus these visas only give you a single entry. You know, in the past they used to provide a one-year visa for postdoctoral students. Anyway, I had such a painful experience getting the visa. I went to the US Consulate twice. The first time, they told me there was something wrong with my I-20 form. They said that my US university had revoked the form. But I called my university and they told me everything was fine. A week later, I went to the Consulate again and they told me they needed to "check" me because of my chemistry background. They told me it would take a month for them to come to a conclusion. Fortunately, I got my visa a week later. But not everyone was as lucky as I was. You know, this is terrifying. Years ago they never checked chemistry-major students. These new policies will have an impact on our lives, our package delivery, our plans to go back home during holidays, etc. So I have already started to question whether I should have come. Now I am thinking perhaps I should go back to China immediately after my PhD.

Ailing's accounts show that even after beginning her overseas studies she is still deciding where to stay and for how long. For her, decision-making about overseas studies is an ongoing process, not a one-time event.

Hong: **Family as Both Push and Pull**

Hong is a 38-year-old senior product manager at a leading United States high-tech firm. She graduated with an MBA from an elite private US university in 2015. When she discusses her motivations for studying abroad, she emphasizes the gravitational pull of her husband and the push from her parents. She worked as a manager at another US firm in China before the MBA. Limited room for personal development also contributed to her decision to change life courses.

Hong's husband came to the United States 2 years before she applied for her MBA. She considers joining her husband the most important pull from the United States:

> *My husband grew up in a family where his parents always talked about how great democracy was in the US....He also talks a lot about Western ideas like freedom, democracy and individual choice. In the beginning, I did not take these ideas seriously. I wasn't really very interested in coming to the US. But then he came to the US a few years before I did, so we were living separately. We were married before he came. We surely did not want to continue like that. I mean he was determined to come and stay in the US. I figured that I had to move if we still wanted to stay together.*

When asked whether the move had meant sacrificing in her career, Hong clarifies that overseas studies had proven to be her opportunity to change job tracks. She explains the regard for elite MBA programs among high-tech firms as an indispensable pull factor for the United States. By her account below, the lack of opportunity in her previous position in China also serves as a push factor for her home country:

> *I was a sales manager in a US company's Beijing office. I wasn't really into sales. I was more interested in marketing. But it was difficult to switch to the marketing team without relevant experience or a degree. I also noticed that it was very difficult to get promoted in our department. It was pretty clear that those with MBA degrees were on the fast track to promotion. You know, our company was an American tech firm. An MBA degree from an elite university in the US is what people expect when promotion comes up. So basically I knew there wasn't too much to give up (if I left). After the MBA, I changed to marketing and the transition was smooth.*

Of course, leaving China during its rapid economic growth invokes economic and opportunity costs for a manager. Not every manager, however, necessarily considers economic prosperity as a pull of the home country. It is often through the framing and interpretation of family members and friends that such pull factors are felt. Hong explains,

> *Sure there are tremendous costs and uncertainties when you decide to leave your old job and your country. Looking back, housing costs in China have more than tripled since we left. Some of our friends have become millionaires (through owning and selling properties). Can you believe that? ... But again, I did not think too much about these things. I was thinking about how to be together with my husband. I was thinking about how to land a job I liked better. I wasn't paying much attention to other things. My father thought of these factors more than I did. I remember he even sent me a message asking me to think twice. He thought it would be a big loss to give up my three hundred thousand RMB annual salary there (in China). He was dubious that I could find a good job in the US. And I was like, "OK, perhaps I should think a little bit about that."*

Clearly, Hong's family members have successfully framed the economic gains associated with the previous position as a pull of the home country. On the other hand, her family serves as a factor that pushes her out of her home country. In light of extensive parental control over children's lives in China, students do not necessarily consider leaving their parents to be unbearably painful. As Hong suggests,

> You would think Chinese people always want to live close to their parents, right? That may be true for many Chinese. I have a different opinion on this issue. My mother is a middle-school math teacher. She likes giving orders on everything I do, like what to wear, what food to eat, what to study and who to befriend. I mean we have not lived together since my college years. But every time I go back home for holidays or other things, she still treats me like a child. So honestly, I don't mind living a bit far away from my parents. I mean we will still go back and visit them for sure. By the way, my father used to be in the army. I did not see him much even when I was young. So we aren't very close anyway.

Hong's comments do not mean that she does not care about her parents. Neither does she want to remain away from them forever. To her, leaving China for overseas studies is like adding a temporary cushion between her and her parents.

Hong's words also emphasize the importance of alumni networks. In her case, her schoolmates had not explicitly encouraged her to study abroad. However, she had been under pressure to compare herself to her former schoolmates. She also views their life trajectories as a benchmark to discovering what her next step should be:

> I definitely miss my best friends in Beijing who were also my fellow college students. We were really close, especially when my husband was away. But in general, I would say my college experience and classmates made me realize I wanted to leave China…There are two groups of people that are relevant here. One of them consists mostly of guys. Many of them are working on their own startups in China. Some are now millionaires. But when I looked at how they lived their lives, you know, going to parties all night long and hanging out with businessmen, I didn't see myself…Another group includes many of my college friends who studied overseas right after graduation. You know, there are a lot of them because I was in a computer science program. Quite a few of them are now professors in the US and Canada. There are also managers living in Silicon Valley. I looked at their Facebook pictures and I said to myself, "this is more or less like how I want to live". It is not that they live a rich life. You look at their family pictures and you just feel that their lives are peaceful.

In this case, her alumni network is both a push and a pull factor. While those with corporate lifestyles had discouraged Hong from pursuing a business career in China, the peaceful lives of her schoolmates in the United States were attractive to her.

In addition to the above-mentioned factors, Hong points to the roles of test-preparation schools in China. These schools prepare Chinese students for standardized tests such as the TOEFL, GRE, and the Graduate Management Admission Test (GMAT). Like family and alumni networks, these organizations also act as interpreters for push and pull factors. Hong describes how these organizations and their classes shaped her perceptions about the United States, MBAs and her decision to study overseas:

> I mentioned to you that I decided to come to the US because of my husband. But I had thought about overseas studies at an earlier time as well. In the summer after my first year in college, I took a GRE class at Supernova School (pseudonym) in Beijing. I went there because lots of my college classmates were going there too. Before going there, I actually knew very little about studying abroad. I did not even know what test to take. I just signed up for what was popular with my classmates. At Supernova, I got lots of new information. For example, I heard about MBA and the GMAT for the first time. I heard about many great

US universities. I remember they (people at Supernova) organized free information sessions for students. One Supernova teacher came to share his experience. He had gotten a Yale MBA and come back to work for Supernova. I still remember how he described his MBA experience. He said, "It was like riding a helicopter. Before the MBA, we looked at business problems as if we were on the ground. But after the MBA, we were able to develop a birds-eye view." You know, it was something like that. So I guess his sharing planted this seed in me.

Apparently, these test-preparation schools not only disseminate information about the United States and the application process; they also promulgate the academic prestige of US universities. In other words, they frame US education into a pull of the host country. This framing made US education more appealing.

In addition to framing the pull of host countries, these test-preparation schools also mitigate difficulties involved in test taking. As mentioned in the previous case, preparing for and participating in standardized tests are considered time-consuming and risky. Thus, these tasks are perceived as barriers for overseas studies. Test-preparation schools reduced this barrier by familiarizing students with information and skills for tests. More importantly, these test-preparation schools build new communities for students to prepare for tests. Hong contextualizes this idea:

It would be hard to imagine going through the test preparation and applications without these schools. Of course, the so-called test skills they teach are not really very useful. But the teachers are encouraging. They tell stories about how other students fight to go abroad. So sometimes their classes were only two hours but I would go back home and study for another twenty hours... Another thing is that these schools help students form a community. This is a group of people with common interests. After the class ends, we still kept in touch about how to prepare for tests and how to apply. When I felt tired or when I was stuck, I would reach out to them.

Concluding Remarks

This chapter draws on individual decision-making processes to enhance understanding of the push–pull framework introduced in earlier chapters. The stories provided by three overseas Chinese students support the validity of the push–pull framework. I find that multiple push and pull factors mentioned in earlier studies have shaped students' decisions over whether and where to study.

These crucial push and pull factors include, but are not limited to, the academic prestige of the host country and the competition pressure of the home country. In all three informants' stories, the academic superiority of US universities is a gravitational pull of the host country. With regard to the competitive pressure in China, two informants illustrate how it can push students outward: one informant considers the mounting pressure in high school a significant determinant for her study-abroad choice. Another informant lists the unlikelihood of a promotion at work as a crucial consideration for obtaining a professional degree from an elite US university.

The informants' stories also provide new patterns that can be interpreted within the existing push and pull framework. One pattern that stands out in their stories is that few people consider the developed economic status of the United States to be a pull of the host country. A plausible explanation is that, given the rapid economic growth of China, especially for the majority of overseas students who come from urban areas, the United States is no longer economically attractive. Also absent in their stories is the political discourse: except for Hong's husband, no one mentioned democracy, human rights or any other political factors as pulls of Western host countries. This lack of political consideration might be due to the fact that there are no humanities or social sciences students in the sample. Another pattern across the three stories is how decision-makers can translate one push–pull factor into another. When decision-makers have determined their priorities (e.g., academic excellence), they can translate what previously seems to be a pull or push factor in the opposite direction.

This chapter's findings also suggest new directions for improving the existing push–pull framework. Existing studies under the push–pull framework often assume that nation states' push and pull factors shape the decision-making process like objective forces. Moving beyond this assumption, this chapter illustrates that students are also exposed to how push and pull factor are interpreted and framed by test-preparation schools, educational consulting firms and alumni networks. Thus, the ways in which a pull or push factor is depicted and interpreted are no less important than its true nature.

Another area of improvement in the push–pull framework lies in conceptualizing the decision-making process. Most studies using the push–pull framework examine decision-making as if students and their parents reach a final conclusion after comparing the costs and benefits. The premise is that decision-makers do not change their minds once the decision is made. In reality, decision-makers participate in a process that is fluid and complicated: they constantly change their positions, second-guess themselves, and even justify problematic past decisions. In such cases, what was formerly known as a push might be re-interpreted as a pull and vice versa.

References

Findlay, A., Prazeres, L., McCollum, D., & Packwood, H. (2017). "It was always the plan": International study as "learning to migrate". *Area, 49*(2), 192–199.

Iannelli, C., & Huang, J. (2014). Trends in participation and attainment of Chinese students in UK higher education. *Studies in Higher Education, 39*(5), 805–855.

Kondakci, Y. (2011). Student mobility reviewed: Attraction and satisfaction of international students in Turkey. *Higher Education, 62*(5), 573–592.

Li, M., & Bray, M. (2007). Cross-border flows of students for higher education: Push–pull factors and motivations of Mainland Chinese students in Hong Kong and Macau. *Higher Education, 53*(6), 791–818.

Lin, L. (2020). The visible hand behind study-abroad waves: cram schools, organizational framing and the international mobility of Chinese students. *Higher Education, 79* (2), 259–274.

Mazzarol, T., & Soutar, G. N. (2002). "Push-pull" factors influencing international student destination choice. *International Journal of Educational Management, 16*(2), 82–90.

Park, E. L. (2009). Analysis of Korean students' international mobility by 2-D model: Driving force factor and directional factor. *Higher Education, 57*(6), 741–755.

Tan, J. (2013). Introduction. *The international mobility of students in Asia and the Pacific.* Retrieved from the UNESCO website.https://teams.unesco.org/ORG/fu/bangkok/public_events/Shared%20Documents/EISD/HigherEducation/Resources-Publications/The%20International%20Mobility%20of%20Students%20in%20AP.pdf

Chapter 6
Social Stratification and Studying Overseas: Empirical Evidence from Middle Schools in Beijing

Introduction

The outflow of Chinese students interacts with the already rapidly changing class structure in China and how the increasing international mobility of Chinese students would contribute to the social stratification in China remains an important question. The goal of this chapter is to examine the correlations between family backgrounds (i.e., socioeconomic status) and middle-school students' opportunity (i.e., willingness and plan) to study overseas, and how those students differ in their motives in studying overseas depending on the social strata they belong to.

This chapter begins with a discussion of the relevant theoretical backgrounds, including an overview of the social stratification theory and its application in the Chinese context, with a special emphasis on the Effectively Maintained Inequality framework. The methodology is then presented, covering the sample and research design. Next are the findings and discussion, which is followed by concluding remarks.

Theoretical Background

Education—A Transformer or Perpetuator of Social Inequality?

Social inequality, which is "the condition whereby people have unequal access to valued resources, services, and positions in the society" (Kerbo, 2011, p. 9), existed from the very beginning of the history of human societies, often because people are

An earlier version of this chapter was published as the following journal article:
Fan, A., & Cheng, B. (2018). Social stratification and studying overseas: Empirical evidence from middle schools in Beijing. *The Asia-Pacific Education Researcher*, 27(1), 11–21.

differentiated by their individual traits and social roles. When inequality is institutionalized, which means that "there is a system of social relationships that determines who gets what, and why" (Kerbo, 2011, p. 10), social stratification occurs. According to Weber, in all societies, people are stratified into a hierarchy of positions largely based on three "scarce and desired" things, namely, "property, or rights over goods and services; power, or the ability to secure one's way in life even against opposition; and prestige, or social honor" (Tumin, 1985, p. 1). Education, as an element in the prestige/honor assigned to occupations, is often treated as a source of honor in itself. As technology advances and societies industrialize, the elites are forced into greater reliance on technical experts, and thus part of the authority is delegated from the elites to people with knowledge and skills needed to run the vast industrial enterprise. As a result, in industrial and postindustrial societies, knowledge and education have become more important than ownership of property or wealth in determining a person's life chances (Lenski, 1984; Thurow, 1991). In this sense, education has a transformational function in relation to social mobility (Firebaugh & Frank, 1994; Neilsen, 1994).

However, this transformational function of education is restrained because of its high correlation with family backgrounds. As Mare (1981) pointed out, "[i]n most societies, formal schooling is a scarce and unequally distributed resource and a key way through which parents transmit their socioeconomic levels, values, political behaviors, and lifestyles to their offspring" (p. 72).

The relationship between education and social stratification has long been studied. Two important frameworks that have been put forward to explain this relationship are Maximally Maintained Inequality (MMI) and Effectively Maintained Inequality (EMI). Based on a study of the transition to secondary school for the 1908–1956 cohorts in Ireland, Raftery and Hout (1993) put forward the framework of Maximally Maintained Inequality (MMI), which means that transition rates and inequality (as measured by odds-ratio between social origins and educational transitions) remain constant unless forced to change by increasing enrollments. Further, only when the demand for a given level of education reaches saturation for the upper classes will the effect of social backgrounds on the opportunity for that level of education decline over time (Lucas, 2001, 2009).

Unlike MMI, which argues that the effect of family backgrounds only declines when the demand of the upper classes for a certain level of education become universal and thus the benefit of the expansion of educational opportunity can spill over to lower classes, EMI argues that due to the differential in quantity as well as quality of educational opportunity, the upper classes can always resort to their socioeconomic advantages to maintain inequality in educational opportunity. As Lucas (2001) argues,

.... socioeconomically advantaged actors secure for themselves and their children some degree of advantage wherever advantages are commonly possible. On the one hand, if quantitative differences are common, the socioeconomically advantaged will obtain quantitative advantage; on the other hand, if qualitative differences are common the socioeconomically advantaged will obtain qualitative advantage (p. 1652).

The Chinese Context

Social Stratification in China

Accompanying the rapid economic development and the establishment of market as the dominating force for allocating resources, China has been undergoing social transformation which is characterized by rapid social stratification during the past several decades. Social relations in China have undergone great changes since the implementation of the Reform and Opening-up Policy in 1978, marked by the transformation of a rather egalitarian society into a rapidly stratified one based on professional status, income, and wealth. As Li (2008) summarizes: "The mechanism and content of social stratification during the Post-Reform era differ fundamentally from the era prior to the Reform. Social stratification used to be determined by political factors whereas after the Reform political factors declined as driving force of social stratification, and in their place were economic factors. This change is one of the main characteristics of social structure in China" (p. 51).

The Reform and Opening-up Policy is characterized by the marketization of economy, and it allows those who can get rich first. As a result, the previously dominating egalitarian principle of distribution was replaced by the principle of "efficiency first." The first group of people who rode with the tides of market economy accumulated a considerable amount of wealth and became the "riche nouveau" of China, thus breaking the old, flat structure of low income and wealth, and starting the formation of a pyramid structure. Another characteristic of the social changes brought out by the Reform is the increasing importance of capital income over labor income, which further exacerbated the gap between the rich and poor. It is widely recognized that 0.4 is the danger line for the Gini Coefficient, the most widely used indicator for income distribution, as it indicates that social wealth has concentrated in the hands of a minority of people, and research has shown the Gini Coefficient increased from 0.32 in 1985 to 0.48 in 2008 in China (Chen & Zhou, 2002; Hu, Liu, & Gong, 2011).

According to Xueyi Lu (2002), a renowned sociologist in China, Chinese society can be divided into ten major strata: (1) unemployed, (2) farmer, (3) industrial worker, (4) staff in business and service sectors, (5) self-employed business owners, (6) clerical staff, (7) professionals and specialists, (8) private business owners, (9) managerial staff, and (10) civil servants and leaders. Among the ten strata, the first three are considered the lower ones, numbers 4 and 5 are the lower-middle, number 6 is the middle, numbers 7 and 8 are the upper-middle, and numbers 9 and 10 are the upper ones. Based on empirical research and data analysis, he concluded that the number of population in each stratum accounted for 3.1%, 44%, 22.6%, 12%, 4.2%, 4.8%, 5.1%, 0.6%, 1.5%, and 2.1%, respectively. In 2010, Lu and his research team did a follow-up study on the social structure in China and found that the classification they had developed earlier still applies, but the percentage of each stratum had changed. More specifically, the largest change lies in the increase in the number of white-collar workers and professionals, civil servants, and private business owners, which all belong to the rising "middle class." The number of the middle class increased at an average rate of 1% each year after 2000. For example, with the national policy of encouraging innovation and entrepreneurship in recent years, medium- and small-sized enterprises have been developing rapidly, and the strata of private business owners expanded accounting for 2.3% of the whole population. Further, as one of the largest group of beneficiaries of the Reform, this social stratum has continuously enhanced the economic, social, and cultural capital at its disposal (Lu, 2010).

Effectively Maintained Inequality (EMI) and Education in China

In rapidly transforming societies, the relationship between education and social inequality is further complicated by the increasingly important role of family background. A review done by Buchmann and Emily (2001) shows that studies in the United States and Great Britain in the 1960s and 1970s concluded that family background was more important than school-related factors in determining student's achievement, whereas later studies done in developing countries concluded that school-related factors played a more significant role in determining students' academic achievement than family background does. Arnove (2013) summarizes the seeming discrepancy as follows:

> Schools do matter, but perhaps to a greater extent in less industrialized countries. Cross-national data over time indicate that as societies industrialize and social class formation solidifies, socioeconomic status becomes increasingly important in determining access to the highest levels of an education system and the most prestigious institutions of learning and to better jobs (p. 5).

China has followed this pattern during the past three decades: As social transformation continues and social stratification solidifies, family background seems to play an increasingly important role in determining students' access to education, choice of institutions, as well as employment opportunities. For example, in China, even though the original intention of expanding higher education on the government's part was to provide more opportunities to postsecondary education institutions for all social groups, research has shown that students from advantaged family backgrounds are overrepresented in more selective institutions. In other words, this differential in the quality of education (as reflected in the selectivity of institutions) becomes the tool for advantaged social groups to maintain their advantages by seeking the rare resources of high-quality education, thus resulting in continuous educational and social inequality. As Li's research (2003, 2014) has shown, in spite of the continuous increase in the quantity of educational opportunities in China since the late 1970s, educational inequality has risen at the same time.

There is consensus among scholars and researchers that social stratification has taken roots in China: Some groups in certain professions and with certain levels of education enjoy certain privileges while others are disadvantaged in the distribution of social resources. The purpose of this study is not to argue about the legitimacy of class differentiation, but to examine the differential in the choice of and access to such educational resources as studying overseas among different social strata, as well as how the differential affects their choice of options in seeking their superior position and thus maintaining the intergenerational transmission of their advantages.

Methodology

Sample

The data used in this study were collected from nine public middle schools located in three different districts of Beijing between June and July 2015. To maximize the representation of the sample, the nine selected schools come from different tiers including municipal key school, district key school, and regular (non-key) school (in descending order of prestige and teaching staff/facilities). For the 2014–2015 academic year, there were a total of 101,045 middle-school graduates in Beijing, and using a 1% sampling criterion, 1300 participants from the graduating class (9th graders)[1] were selected to do the survey, and 1012 valid surveys were returned, resulting in a response rate of 77.85%. The survey included information on students' demographics, socioeconomic status, plans regarding studying overseas, reasons for and concerns over studying overseas, perceived costs and benefits of studying overseas. Considering that in China at the young age of 14–15, those 9th graders are not mature or independent enough to make their own decisions about future academic and career plans, their parents were asked to complete the survey. Among the 1012 respondents, 447, or 44.2% are male students, and the rest are female students.

Research Design

There are two main categories of factors affecting students' decision-making in studying overseas, namely, individual and family characteristics. Individual characteristics include such demographic factors as sex and age, as well as academic achievement.

Participants' family backgrounds are examined from three aspects, namely, social capital, human capital, and economic capital, which roughly correspond to parental profession, parental education, and family income and wealth. And those

---

[1] Chinese secondary schools have a 3 + 3 structure, which means that middle schools cover seventh through ninth grades, and high schools cover ninth through 12th grades.

three forms of capital are among important indicators for a family's socioeconomic status. In analyzing students' family backgrounds, we decided to use father's education and profession instead of mother's. The reason is that in China, which is still a quite patriarchal society, men are still at an advantageous position compared to women, and for most families, the father's social status and professional position determine the family's wealth, social network as well as the amount of resources they could mobilize.

Research has shown that parental profession determines a family's social capital, affecting the social connections and networks the family possesses that could be put to use when making important family decisions. In coding father' profession, we follow the ten categories established by the above-mentioned Lu (2002; 2010), which group the following professions as "upper class": (10) civil servants and leaders, (9) managerial staff, and (8) private business owners; the following professions as "middle class": (7) professionals and specialists, (6) clerical staff, (5) self-employed business owners, and (4) staff in business and service sectors; and the following professions as "lower class": (3) industrial worker, (2) farmer, and (1) unemployed. Two social groups have caught attention in recent years among the public, in the media, as well as among scholars and researchers, and they are labeled "*fuerdai*" and "*guanerdai*," which refer to the offspring of government officials and wealthy business people, respectively. Showered with inherited privilege of power and wealth, those children carry important labels of new social strata (Zhang, 2013). The analysis of this chapter pays particular attention to those groups which are at an advantage in building networks and mobilizing social resources, namely, high-ranking officials (will be referred to as "Official" hereafter), wealthy business owners ("Business" hereafter), and white-collar professionals ("Professional" hereafter). Children of those three groups are examined in reference to others in order to have a more nuanced understanding of how father's profession, along with the economic, human, and social capital associated with it, is correlated with students' willingness and plan to study overseas. Those three subgroups of students are likely to enjoy more social resources because of their fathers' advantaged social status and thus differ from students of other strata in their willingness and plan to study overseas, and examining their opportunity to study overseas may provide a better explanation of how the opportunity to study overseas is related to intergenerational transmission of social inequality.

Parental education is a measure of a family's human capital, and it also reflects the cultural capital of the family. Parents with higher educational level are likely to have higher expectation of their children and are more involved in their children's education, which can all have positive impact on their children's academic achievement and professional accomplishment. They are more willing to seek the best education possible for their children, and when they see studying overseas as a better option for their children, they would send their children overseas even if it means high cost and low-to-no returns on their educational investment. Oftentimes in educational research, mother's education is used in predicting children's academic achievement. This study chose to use father's education for two reasons. One is that mother's and father's educational levels are highly correlated in the data ($r = 0.78$,

$p < 0.01$), and the other is since we are examining families' decision-making instead of children's academic achievement, fathers tend to play a more important role in determining the resources a family could mobilize in making this kind of decisions.

Economic capital is measured by two indicators—family income and family wealth, and family wealth is measured by the number of housing property owned by the family. Given that the average per capita income in Beijing was 77,560 Yuan (an equivalent of $12,510) in 2014, we categorized those with a family income below 100,000 Yuan (an equivalent of $16,129) as low-income family, and those between 100,000 and 300,000 Yuan as middle-income family, and those above 300,000 Yuan (an equivalent of $48,387) as high-income families.

Findings and Discussions

Family Socioeconomic Status of Participants

Table 6.1 summarizes the characteristics of the family backgrounds of the participants. Around half of the sample comes from the three relatively advantaged social groups; more specifically, there are 55 (5.43%) from Official families, 265 (26.19%) from Business families, 191 (18.87%) from Professional families, and the remaining 501 (49.51%) from Other, less advantaged families ($N = 1012$). In terms of fathers' educational backgrounds, 534 (53.61%) of them have received postsecondary education, among which 103 (10.34%) hold graduate degrees ($N = 996$). In addition, 2.3% of the fathers have received their degrees overseas. Regarding family income, 414 (44.37%) students belong to low-income family, 345 (36.98%) belong

Table 6.1 Summary statistics of family backgrounds of participants

	Categories	Number	N
Father's profession	Official	55 (5.43)	1012
	Business	265 (26.19)	
	Professional	191 (18.87)	
	Other	501 (49.51)	
Father's education	High school and below	462 (46.39)	996
	Associate and BA	431 (43.27)	
	Graduate degree	103 (10.34)	
Family income	Low-level	414 (44.37)	933
	Middle-level	345 (36.98)	
	High-level	174 (18.65)	
No. of property owned	None	173 (17.93)	965
	1	464 (48.08)	
	2	231 (23.94)	
	3 and above	97 (10.05)	

Note: Percentages are in parentheses

Table 6.2 Father's education, by social strata

| Social strata | Year of education | | Father's education | | | Total |
	Mean	Median	High school and below	Associate and BA	Graduate degree	
Official	16.59	16	5 (9.3)	33 (61.1)	16 (29.6)	54
Business	13.85	15	118 (44.7)	114 (43.2)	32 (12.1)	264
Professional	15.80	16	36 (19.1)	117 (62.2)	35 (18.6)	188
Other	12.75	12	303 (61.8)	167 (34.1)	20 (4.1)	490

Note: Percentages are in parenthesis

to middle-income family, and 174 (18.65%) belong to high-income family ($N = 933$). As for family wealth, only 173 (17.93%) students' families do not own a housing, 464 (48.08%) of them own one housing, 231 (23.94%) own two properties, and 97 (10.05%) own three properties or above ($N = 965$). The relatively privileged family backgrounds of the participants reflect the relatively high family socioeconomic status of residents in Beijing, the national capital, which has the highest concentration of high-income population with high educational level and high professional status.

Among the four social strata, participants differ in their sociocultural and economic capital, which are respectively measured by father's education, and family income/property. As demonstrated in Table 6.2, the average educational level is the highest for Official (16.59 years), followed by Professional (15.80 years), and then by Business (13.85 years), and the Other stratum has the lowest level (12.75 years). The majority of the Other stratum (61.8%) received high school education and below while for the three advantaged social strata, the majority of them received higher education. The advantage for the Official and Professional strata in this aspect is especially evident: 29.6% of the father in the Official stratum obtained graduate degree, and the number is 18.6% for the Professional stratum. In other words, the Other stratum enjoys the least advantage in sociocultural capital, and among the three advantaged strata, the Official stratum has the largest advantage, followed by Professional, and then Business.

In terms of economic capital, which is measured by family income and number of housing property owned, the Business and Official strata seem to enjoy the largest advantage, as demonstrated in Tables 6.3 and 6.4. The average annual family income is the highest for the Business stratum (328,000 Yuan—an equivalent of $52,903), followed by Official (294,200 Yuan—an equivalent of $47,452) and then by Professional (223,000 Yuan—an equivalent of $35,968), and the Other stratum has the lowest income (170,300 Yuan—an equivalent of $27,468). The Business and Official strata also have the highest percentage of high-income families (34.3% and 32.7%, respectively). As for family wealth, the Official stratum owns the highest number of housing property on average (1.41), followed by Business (1.38), and then by Professional (1.30), and the Other stratum owns the lowest number of housing property (1.16). The Official and Business strata also have the highest percentage of families possessing three housing properties and above (15.7% and 14.0%,

Table 6.3 Family income, by social strata (in 10,000 Yuan)

Social strata	Family income				
	Mean	Low	Middle	High	Total
Overall	22.75	414 (44.4)	345 (37.0)	174 (18.6)	933
Official	29.42	8 (15.4)	27 (51.9)	17 (32.7)	52
Business	32.80	58 (24.3)	99 (41.4)	82 (34.3)	239
Professional	22.30	48 (27.6)	92 (52.9)	34 (19.5)	174
Other	17.03	300 (64.1)	127 (27.1)	41 (8.8)	468

Note: Percentages are in parenthesis

Table 6.4 Number of housing owned by the family, by social strata

Social strata	No. of housing property owned				
	Mean	None	1	2	3 and above	Total
Overall	1.26	173 (17.9)	464 (48.1)	231 (23.9)	97 (10.1)	965
Official	1.41	9 (17.6)	20 (39.2)	14 (27.5)	8 (15.7)	51
Business	1.38	48 (18.6)	100 (38.3)	74 (28.7)	36 (14.0)	258
Professional	1.30	25 (13.6)	90 (48.9)	57 (31.0)	12 (6.5)	184
Other	1.16	91 (19.3)	254 (53.8)	86 (18.2)	41 (8.7)	472

Note: Percentages are in parenthesis

respectively). Even though the Official stratum has a slightly lower average annual income than the Business stratum, their profession may bring resources that can be transformed into family wealth. For example, the average market price for real estate was 25,873 Yuan per square meter (an equivalent of $4173) in Beijing in 2014, but government employees were qualified for subsidized housing at the low price of 10,000 Yuan per square meter (an equivalent of $1613). For a 100-m^2 apartment (an equivalent of 1076 square feet), the price differences could reach 1,500,000 Yuan (an equivalent of $241,935), 9 times as much as the annual family income of the Other stratum, 6.7 times as much as that of the Professional stratum, and 4.6 times as much as that of the Business stratum.

To sum up, the three social strata of Official, Business, and Professional are advantaged than the Other stratum in every aspect, including human, sociocultural as well as economic capital. Among them, the Official and Professional strata seem to enjoy the largest sociocultural capital, and the Official and Business strata enjoy the largest economic capital.

Participants' Plans to Study Overseas

As shown in Fig. 6.1, among the 1012 participants, 299 (29.5%) do not have plans to study overseas, 19 (1.90%) plan to study overseas for high school, 131 (12.90%) for undergraduate, 118 (11.70%) for graduate degrees, and the remaining 445 (44.00%) are uncertain. In analysis, we consider those who are uncertain about

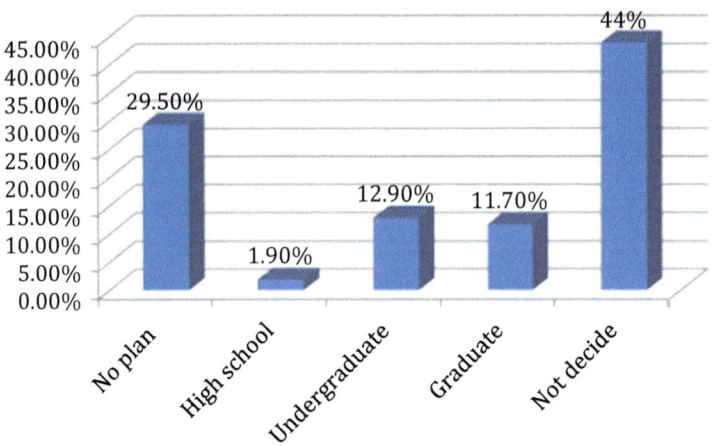

Fig. 6.1 Percentage of participants' plans for studying overseas ($N = 1012$)

Table 6.5 Students' plans regarding studying overseas, by socioeconomic status

| | Not studying overseas | Going overseas | | | | |
		For high school	For undergraduate	For graduate study	Uncertain	N
Overall	299 (29.5)	19 (1.9)	131 (12.9)	118 (11.7)	445 (44)	1012
Official	13 (23.60)	3 (5.50)	10 (18.20)	9 (16.40)	20 (36.40)	55
Business	71 (26.80)	6 (2.30)	57 (21.50)	33 (12.50)	98 (37.00)	265
Professional	41 (21.50)	1 (0.50)	29 (15.20)	37 (19.40)	83 (43.50)	191
Other	174 (34.70)	9 (1.80)	35 (7.00)	39 (7.80)	244 (48.70)	501
Low-income	157 (37.90)	6 (1.40)	24 (5.80)	33 (8.00)	194 (46.90)	414
Middle-income	95 (27.50)	4 (1.20)	37 (10.70)	53 (15.40)	156 (45.20)	345
High-income	28 (16.10)	8 (4.60)	57 (32.80)	25 (14.40)	56 (32.20)	174

Note: Percentages are in parentheses

studying overseas willing to do so. Among the five groups shown in Fig. 6.1, the right four groups are considered open and thus willing to study overseas. It seems that the majority of them—713 (70.5%)—are willing to study overseas although some of them have not made plans yet.

As shown in Table 6.5, children of the three advantaged social strata are more willing to study overseas, and are more likely to have specific plans for studying overseas: Only 26.8% of the Business families, 23.60% of the Official families, and 21.50% of the Professional families do not have intentions to study overseas, as compared to 34.70% in the Other stratum; 40.10% of the Official families, 36.30% of the Business families, and 35.10% of the Professional families have made plans to study overseas, as compared to 16.60% in the Other stratum. In other words, the

Professional families are the most open to the idea of studying overseas while the Official families have made the clearest plans. As for the timing, Official families (18.20%) and Business families (21.5%) seem to favor sending their children overseas for undergraduate study, whereas the Professional families (19.40%) favor graduate study. Even though only 5.50% of the Official families intend to send their children overseas to study for high school, it is a much higher percentage than for the other social strata.

In terms of family income, high-income families are more willing and more likely to have specific plans to send their children to study overseas: Only 16.10% of the high-income families do not consider the option of studying overseas for their children, and the numbers are 27.50% and 37.90% for middle-income and low-income families, respectively; 51.80% of the high-income families have made plans to study overseas, and the numbers are 27.30% and 15.20% for middle-income and low-income families, respectively. As for the timing, high-income families seem to favor sending their children overseas for undergraduate study (32.8%), whereas the middle-income and (15.4%) low-income families (8.0%) seem to favor graduate study. Even though only 4.60% of the high-income families intend to send their children overseas to study for high school, it is a much higher percentage than for middle-income and low-income families.

Participants' Academic Achievement

All middle schools in Beijing conduct a simulation test in May every year, about 2 months before the official high-school-entrance examination. Since this test has been proved to be an accurate predictor of students' performance on the entrance exam, we used students' scores on this test as the proxy for their academic achievement. An analysis of students' performance on the test, as presented in Fig. 6.2,

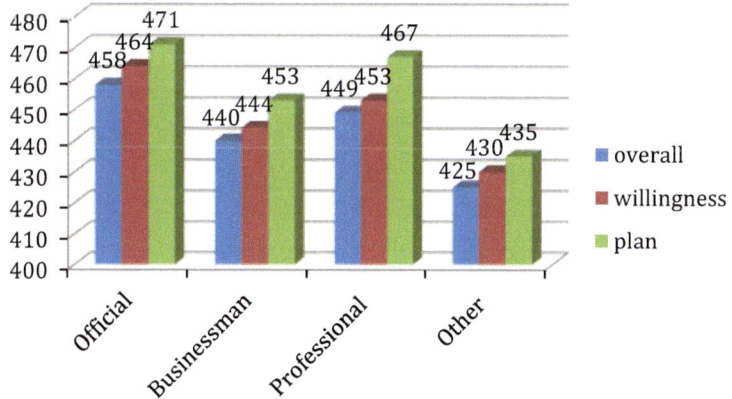

Fig. 6.2 Participants' academic achievement of different social studying overseas, by social strata

shows that children of the Official stratum have the highest score on average (458), followed by the Professional stratum (449), and then by the Business stratum (440), and the Other stratum has the lowest average score (425).

For all social strata, students who have already made plans to study overseas have the highest average score, followed by students who are willing to study overseas. This finding does not necessarily conflict with the public's perception that many students go overseas to pursue study because of their poor academic record. While it is true that some students have to pursue study overseas because they are likely to be screened out by the College-Entrance Examination, the majority of students who are willing and intend to study overseas perform above the average. Further, it can be argued that students who perform better academically tend to have more explicit plans for their future professional development, as supported by other research on college students (Fan & Yang, 2015).

How Social Strata Affect the Opportunity of Studying Overseas

It seems from the above analysis that different social strata differ in their willingness and plans to study overseas. In order to better examine the effect of social strata, logistic regressions were run. In running regressions, we used two dependent variables, namely, Willingness (to study overseas) and Plan (for studying overseas). As stated previously, Willingness includes both those who have made plans to study overseas and those who are uncertain about (and thus open to) studying overseas. Independent variables include such individual characteristics as sex and social strata.

As presented in Table 6.6, there is a positive relationship between students' willingness/plan and each of the three social strata, namely, Official, Business, and

Table 6.6 Logistic regression results

	Willingness		Plan	
	B	Exp (β)	B	Exp (β)
Social strata				
Official	0.59* (0.34)	1.81	1.16*** (0.31)	3.2
Business	0.47*** (0.18)	1.60	1.10*** (0.18)	3.0
Professional	0.67*** (0.20)	2.00	1.0*** (0.20)	2.71
Beijing *Hukou*	0.39* (0.22)	1.48	0.29 (0.23)	1.34
Male	−0.05 (0.14)	0.95	0.18 (0.15)	1.20
Constant	0.28 (0.23)	1.33	−1.94 (0.26)	0.14
−2 log likelihood	1184.92		1102.78	
Observations	991		991	

Note: Standard errors are in parentheses. Reference group for "Social strata" is "other," and reference group for "male" is "female"
*Significant at the 10% level
**Significant at the 5% level
***Significant at the 1% level

Professional. The relationships are statistically significant. Since the Other stratum is used as the reference group, the positive coefficients mean that students from Official, Business, and Professional strata are less likely to reject the idea of studying overseas and more likely to have made plans to study overseas upon graduation from middle school. Among the three relatively advantaged social strata, Professional is the most willing to study overseas and is thus most open to this idea. More specifically, the odds for a student from the Professional stratum is two times as high as the odds for a student from the Other stratum, whereas the numbers are 1.81 and 1.60 for a student from the Official stratum and Business stratum, respectively. In terms of making specific plans to study overseas, students from the Official stratum seem to have the highest odds among the three relatively advantaged social strata. More specifically, the odds for a student from the Official stratum is 3.2 times as high as the odds for a student from the Other stratum, whereas the numbers are 3.0 and 2.71 for a student from the Business stratum and Professional stratum, respectively.

Moreover, sex does not seem to have a statistically significant effect on the Willingness or Plan to study overseas. This is quite different from the high drop-out rates among girls in rural areas. A possible explanation is that parents in cities, with their higher educational level, are less gender biased. Further, 90% of the students in the sample are the only child in their family, and they all, boys or girls, carry their parents' hopes, and thus parents do not discriminate against them in their educational investment.

In order to better examine how students differ within each social stratum, logistic regressions were run separately for each stratum, and the results are presented in Table 6.7. As one can see from Table 6.7, for the Other strata, students' academic achievement seems to play a more important role than it does for the Official, Business, and Professional strata. For the three relatively advantaged social strata, although it varies somewhat among them, it seems that family income is the most important factor. In other words, for students who are not from advantageous family backgrounds, studying overseas could be an option for those with a good academic record, and thus a means for upward social mobility, whereas for those from relatively advantaged family backgrounds, studying overseas has more to do with their family economic capital such as family income, and sociocultural capital such as parents' education.

The logistic regression results seem to support the Effectively Maintained Inequality theory since the more advantaged social strata are more willing to study overseas and more likely to make plans to study overseas. They use studying overseas, which is associated with better educational resources, to maintain their advantageous socioeconomic status. Advantaged social groups can create more educational opportunities for their children. As China went through the transformation from planned economy to market economy, power in policy-making and control over rare resources could bring economic revenues and benefits. Further, those who make and implement policies often own administrative rent-seeking power which allows them to exchange for social services. For example, they can enjoy expensive housing at a very low price, and they can enjoy high-quality medical treatment and their children can have access to high-quality schools, all of which are rare social resources

Table 6.7 Summary of logistic regression results for each social strata

	Official		Business		Professional		Other	
	Willingness	Plan	Willingness	Plan	Willingness	Plan	Willingness	Plan
Family income	1.321**	−0.02	0.01	0.20**	0.08	0.207*	0.03	0.09
No. of housing owned	−0.76	0.12	0.19	0.19	0.34	0.19	0.15	0.34
Father's education	0.19	0.52	0.71**	0.23	−0.306	0.46	−0.04	0.22
Academic achievement	−0.001	0.003	0.000	0.003	0.010**	0.006	0.003*	0.002*
Beijing *Hukou*	−18.85	20.55	0.10	0.02	0.35	−1.38*	0.64	−0.13
Constant	−3.34**	−23.88	−0.57	−1.49	−3.98**	−4.02**	19.19	−3.68**
−2 log likelihood	33.19		249.54		161.7		523.23	
Observations	55		265		191		501	

Note: Standard errors are in parentheses. All models include "sex" as the control

*Significant at the 10% level

**Significant at the 5% level

beyond the reach of ordinary citizens and lower class groups (Ding & Weng, 2015). Chen (2012), based on empirical research, found that parents in high-status professions have significant effect on their children's access to high-quality postsecondary institutions, especially those with political power and connections as they try to maximize the intergenerational transmission of their advantages through power.

The value of administrative power is even more pronounced in elementary and secondary education. In order for their children to have a head-start in the competition for educational opportunities and resources, advantaged social groups often seek out the best schools for their children through their power and connections even though the government has a nearby-enrollment policy which stipulates that students should go to the nearest school in their neighborhood. Wu and Wang (2008), through analyzing the class differentiation of middle-school students in Beijing, found a strong, positive correlation between family income, parental education, parental profession on the one hand, and the quality of school their children attend on the other hand. This shows that even at the 9-year compulsory education level which aims at achieving equity, there is differential in students' access to quality education among different social groups. For high school, which is not compulsory education, Yang (2005) found that in both cities and the countryside, the children of middle- and low-class families are overrepresented in non-key schools while those from higher class family backgrounds are overrepresented in key schools which enjoy more qualified teachers and better facilities. The competition in gaining access to key schools has become the contest of parents' economic and social capital.

Research has also shown that it is through the mechanism of the reproduction of cultural capital that the intergenerational transmission of education is completed. Pan and Han (2015) explains this mechanism as follows: In a test-driven educational system, parents can transmit their cultural capital to their children through expectation, economic investment, and networking, thus improving their children's motives and aspirations. As a result, their opportunity to high-quality education is enhanced.

Concluding Remarks

The increasing number of Chinese students studying abroad accompanies the rising of the so-called middle class, and it is not a mere coincidence. Studying overseas requires financial resources that only those from relatively well-to-do families can afford. In other words, middle and upper social classes have more options for their children, including the opportunity to pursue study overseas. In fact, recent literature on the global mobility of students shows that "by creating new opportunities for differentiation, study abroad may allow already privileged individuals to maintain their class status" (Perkins & Neumayer, 2014, p. 248).

According to Bourdieu (1973; 1977), education is the reproduction of social relations, and under certain social circumstances, professional and social status can be transmitted through education from generation to generation. The EMI framework seems to do a good job explaining what has been happening in China. As stated above, EMI thinks that advantaged social groups will try their best to maximize educational inequality in access as well as quality. When access to education is no longer sufficient in maintaining their advantaged status, they will turn to maximizing the differentiation of the educational quality between them and others by seeking opportunities to the highest-quality education possible.

As demonstrated by this study, education actually has a multifaceted function in society: On the one hand, education is regarded by disadvantaged social groups as the tool for transcending their original class, and on the other hand, it is considered by the privileged social groups as the means to maintaining their privileges. Through analyzing how different social strata differ in their willingness and plan to study overseas, this empirical study has shown that studying overseas, which is considered an option for pursuing high-quality educational resources, has proven to be such a tool for advantaged social class to maintain their status and for disadvantaged social class to climb up the social ladder.

References

Arnove, R. (2013). Introduction: Reframing comparative education: The dialectic of the global and the local. In R. F. Arnove & C. A. Torres (Eds.), *Comparative education: The dialectic of the global and the local*. Lanham, MD: Rowman and Littlefield.

Bourdieu, P. (1973). Cultural reproduction and social reproduction. In R. Brown (Ed.), *Knowledge, education and cultural change*. London: Tavistock Publications.

Bourdieu, P. (1977). *Reproduction in education, society and culture*. London: Sage.

Buchmann, C., & Emily, H. (2001). Education and stratification in developing countries: A review of theories and research. *Annual Review of Sociology, 27*, 77–102.

Chen, X. (2012). Who has the opportunity to enter good universities in China? An empirical study on the distribution of the access to postsecondary institutions of differential quality. *Studies on Higher Education, 2*, 20–29.

Chen, Z., & Zhou, Y. (2002). *Another discussion on income distribution during the reform and development*. Beijing: Economic Science Press.

Ding, X., & Weng, Q. (2015). Professional power and families' educational expenditure: An empirical analysis from a political and economic perspective. *Educational Research, 8*, 33–41.

Fan, A., & Yang, P. (2015). College students' strategies for career readiness: An empirical study based on student development data from universities in Beijing. *Chinese Higher Education Studies, 10*, 95–102.

Firebaugh, G., & Frank, D. B. (1994). Does economic growth benefit the masses: Growth, dependence, and welfare in the third world. *American Sociological Review, 59*, 631–653.

Hu, Z., Liu, Z., & Gong, Z. (2011). An estimate on the Gini coefficient of China's overall income: 1985–2008. *Economics, 3*, 1423–1436.

Kerbo, H. R. (2011). *Social stratification and inequality: Class conflict in historical, comparative, and global perspective* (8th ed.). New York: McGraw Hill.

Lenski, G. E. (1984). *Power and privilege: A theory of social stratification*. Chapel Hill: North Carolina University Press.

Li, C. (2003). Social and political changes and inequality of educational opportunity: The impact of family backgrounds and systemic factors on access to education (1940–2001). *Social Science in China, 3*, 86–98.

Li, C. (2014). Trends and changes of educational inequality (1940–2010): A further examination of the inequality of educational opportunity between the urban and rural. *Sociological Studies, 2*, 65–89.

Li, Q. (2008). The changes of Chinese social stratification structure in the 30 years of reform and opening up. *Social Science of Beijing, 5*, 47–60.

Lu, X. (2002). *A report on the social strata of contemporary China*. Beijing: Social Sciences Academic Press.

Lu, X. (2010). *Social structure in contemporary China*. Beijing: Social Sciences Academic Press.

Lucas, S. R. (2001). Effectively maintained inequality: Education transitions, track mobility, and social background effects. *American Journal of Sociology, 106*(6), 1642–1690.

Lucas, S. R. (2009). Stratification theory, social background, and educational attainment: A formal analysis. *Rationality and Society, 21*(4), 459–511.

Mare, R. D. (1981). Change and stability in educational stratification. *American Sociological Review, 46*, 72–87.

Neilsen, F. (1994). Income inequality and industrial development: Dualism revisited. *American Sociological Review, 59*, 654–677.

Pan, Z., & Han, Y. (2015). The intergenerational transmission of socioeconomic status and the reproduction of inequality: Based on the analysis of the CGSS2011 data. *The Academic Journal of Central South University, 6*, 152–157.

Perkins, R., & Neumayer, E. (2014). Geographies of educational mobilities: Exploring the uneven flows of international students. *The Geographical Journal, 180*(3), 246–259.

Raftery, A. E., & Hout, M. (1993). Maximally maintained inequality: Expansion, reform, and opportunity in Irish education, 1921–75. *Sociology of Education, 66*, 41–62.

Thurow, L. C. (1991). *Head to head: The coming economic battle between the United States, Japan, and Europe*. New York: Morrow.

Tumin, M. M. (1985). *Social stratification: The forms and functions of inequality* (2nd ed.). Englewood Cliffs, NJ: Prentice-Hall.

Wu, C., & Wang, S. (2008). A study on class gap and equity of compulsory education: Based on data from middle schools in Beijing. *Education and Economy, 4*, 1–5.

Yang, D. (2005). Social stratification and access to education in high school. *Qsinghua Journal of Education, 6*, 52–59.

Zhang, J. (2013). *Fuerdai* and *Guanerdai*: Commonalities and differences in the structure of media language. *Modern Communications, 3*, 49–54.

Chapter 7
Adaptations of "Parachute Kids" from China in American High Schools

Introduction

The move to a new culture could be one of the most traumatic experiences in a person's life, and it is often compared to a period of mourning for their home environment, characterized by feelings of grief and separation anxiety (Bock, 1970; Furnham, 1995; Garza-Guerrero, 1974; Kim, 1988). The term "acculturation" is commonly used to study the process of adaptation of those who are placed in a new culture. Redfield, Linton, and Herskovits (1936) presented the classical definition of acculturation: "acculturation comprehends those phenomena which result when groups of individuals having different cultures come into continuous first-hand contact with subsequent changes in the original culture patterns of either or both groups" (p. 149). In other words, it refers to "the cultural changes resulting from these group encounters" (Berry, 1997, p. 6).

Different models have been developed to examine the process of acculturation, including the U-curve and W-curve models (Adler, 1975; Brown, 1980; Gullahourn & Gullahorn, 1960; Lysgaard, 1955; Oberg, 1960). Unlike early research which tended to study adaptation as a unilinear, unidirectional process as they had assumed that immigrants would inevitably be absorbed into their societies of settlement (Gordon, 1964), later research views adaptation as a bi-dimensional process which is related to both their cultures of origin and the receiving societies (Berry, 1974; Phinney, 1990). Under the bi-dimensional concept, Berry proposed four acculturation attitudes and strategies depending on "the degree to which people wish to maintain their heritage culture and identity; and the degree to which people seek involvement with the larger society" (Berry, Phinney, Sam, & Vedder, 2006, p. 306). These four acculturation strategies are: *assimilation*, which is when "individuals do not wish to maintain their cultural identity and seek daily interaction with other cultures"; *separation*, which is when "individuals place a value on holding on to their original culture, and at the same time wish to avoid interaction with others";

B. Cheng et al., *The New Journey to the West*, Education in the Asia-Pacific Region: Issues, Concerns and Prospects 53, https://doi.org/10.1007/978-981-15-5588-6_7

integration, which is when "there is an interest in both maintaining one's original culture, while in daily interactions with other groups"; and *marginalization*, which is "when there is little possibility or interest in cultural maintenance, and little interest in having relations with others" (Berry, 1997, p. 9). Searle and Ward (1990) further distinguished between psychological and sociocultural adaptation in the process of acculturation. The former refers to "feelings of well-being and satisfaction, whereas the latter is concerned with the ability to 'fit in' or negotiate interactive aspects of the host culture" (Ward & Kennedy, 1993, p. 131).

Parachute Kids and Adaptation

As mentioned in Chap. 1, "parachut kids" is a term used to describe unaccompanied minors, unaccompanied sojourners, or little overseas students from Asian regions such as Taiwan, Hong Kong, South Korea, Malaysia, Indonesia and mainland China, who are dropped off in the U.S. to go to school while their parents stay in their country of origin. If the process of acculturation is difficult for any international sojourner, it is only more difficult for parachute kids. The interface between cultural adjustments and individual development more than double the difficult task of acculturation for them. While still in the stage of forming their identities, which is a difficult task for any teenager, they have to do it among all the uncertainties brought by the new cultural environment and without the daily support of their family. As Tsong and Liu (2008) stated: "The changes associated with immigration and separation from one or both parents make the challenges that come with normative developmental tasks in this age group all the more difficult" (p. 370). Cheng (2019) reveals adjustments can be made at three levels, namely, tangible, structural and mental ones. An example of a tangible adjustment is the need for a sense of home and belonging; structural adjustments include teacher-student relationships and interpersonal relationships; and mental adjustments include the change from being privileged to being disadvantaged, and from being passive to being proactive.

As demonstrated in the three stories in this chapter, those who are integrated appear to be those with an open and curious mind, who are proactive in making adjustments by getting to know more about the local people and culture, and who use the adjustments as an opportunity for reflection and growth, as is the case of *Rong*. In contrast, those who resist making adjustments appear to be those with a more passive attitude who thus become separated from the host culture, as is the case of *Fen*. The majority of them seem to fall between: They do not resist the new culture while holding onto their home culture, but at the same time, they struggle to reconcile the differences. They are willing to make some adjustments, but not at deeper levels. In other words, in between separation and integration are those who are still exploring ways to navigate between two cultures, as is the case of *Zhong*.

Rong: A Case of Integration

Rong was a high school senior at the time of the interview, and she struck me as an independent, mature, and thoughtful person. In fact, the maturity and thoughtfulness she demonstrated throughout the interview, I would say, exceeded my expectation of a 19-year-old girl. I would even go as far as saying that she symbolizes the kind of transformation I would hope for every international student, which enabled her to be well integrated with the host culture and society.

Among the interviews I did with students, she was the only one who had proactively suggested to her parents the idea of studying overseas. All the other students had been forced, persuaded, or told by their parents to study overseas. Even though there were a few other students who welcomed the idea of studying overseas, and thus did not need any persuasion from their parents, *Rong* was the only one who had to persuade her parents to agree to send her to study overseas.

During the 4 years she had studied in American high schools, she actively seized opportunities to enrich herself. While maintaining a high GPA throughout high school, she had joined the theater team, the speech and debate team and also had done Model United Nations. Despite (or because of) being under constant pressure and having often to work until midnight, she had a highly fulfilling and rewarding high school experience. All her efforts had paid off, and she was admitted to an ivy-league college by the time she was interviewed.

Rong came from a provincial capital city located in central China. Her father ran a private business, and her mother was a housewife. Both parents had a college degree. She described her family atmosphere as "open" since her parents tended to respect her decisions.

The summer before entering middle school, she went on a study tour to a summer camp in Australia and the United States. During the one month she spent in New York, she met many students from all over the world and participated in various activities, including sports such as water polo. Those "fun" and "cool" experiences on the study tour opened her mind and sowed the seeds for the idea of studying in the United States. In the meantime, starting from the 6th grade until the 8th grade, her mother took her to a local club on a regular basis. She described the club as similar to a coffee house, where she could practice English with native English speakers, and she made some friends from other countries there. The experiences at the club further opened her mind, and stimulated her interest in studying overseas.

She had studied in a top middle school before going overseas although she described herself as an "average student" in that school. During the last year of middle school (the equivalent of 9th grade in the US), motivated by the pressure to get into a good high school, she worked so hard that she became one of the top three students in her class. Her parents, convinced by her determination and seeing her potential, decided to support her idea of studying overseas. They later told her that they were reluctant to send her to study overseas because they knew it would not be an easy life, and they did not want her to suffer. However, having witnessed her stamina and pioneering spirit, they decided to "release her to the outside world to try for herself." Her parents helped her choose the destination state in the United States because they had friends in that state. Her parents' friends also recommended a catholic girls' college preparatory school, and she repeated the 9th grade there. After one year at this girls' school, she transferred to a larger co-ed private school not far away, and that's where she spent the remaining three years in high school.

Prior to arriving in the United States, she had envisioned an easy and happy high school life where the atmosphere was free and people were nice, as depicted in American movies and shows that she had watched in China. Interestingly, there seems to be a common perception among Chinese students, prior to their arrival in the United States, that American schools are easy. It is an idea widely publicized in Chinese schools which proves to be one of the biggest myths about American schools among Chinese students. As *Rong* soon found out, academic pressure was actually pretty high in American schools, and people in the United States were not as nice as they were in movies. During the first year in the US high school, she felt great pressure in both study and life. Difficulty in study was partially due to language barrier, and adaptation in life was made more difficult because of the tension with the host family. Being a perfectionist who did not like to be considered any lesser added to her stress and anxiety. Even though, thanks to her prior experiences of study tour to Australia and the United States, as well as her preparation in English such as the practice at the club, her English had reached the level of proficiency, she could not express herself as freely in English as she did in Chinese and thus felt limited. Further, she did not like the accent in her pronunciation. The first month was the most difficult time for her as she had never felt so lost before, and even the things that were commonplace to American students, such as a group project, she could not fully understand what she was supposed to do. It was as if all her 15 years of learning had been removed, and this feeling of loss and ignorance dealt a heavy blow to her confidence.

She felt many other restraints. For example, the living arrangement of staying with a host family meant that she could not invite her friends over as she wanted and that she needed a ride to go anywhere. She felt further restrained because she could not express herself as freely as she wanted to, especially when it came to subtleties. All those contributed to her feeling of being restrained.

After one month or so, she was able to understand the requirements of assignments, and gradually she was able to catch up and even exceeded many students. To her surprise, she received the highest score in her English class at the end of the first year. To this impressive accomplishment, she did not show any complacency or even satisfaction at the interview. Instead, she shrugged her shoulder: You know, that was a small school and their academic level was not that high.

Rong's mom was with her in the host family during her first year in the United States, which helped to ease the adaptation, especially the adjustments needed in life, including how to get along with the host family. Her host family was of Japanese descent, and they had many house rules that *Rong* was not used to and did not like. For example, she was not allowed to take a shower after 10:30 pm. Further, she had to help with the house chores, which is required in the *Host Family Handbook* issued by the school. She did not like to help clean up after dinner which could take as long as half an hour and would rather use this time to do homework. The host family was also direct in pointing out *Rong*'s mistake or things that they did not think *Rong* did appropriately. It took some time for both sides to adjust, and toward the end of the first year, they all got along, and she had been staying with the same host family for the following 3 years.

Also different from her expectations was that she found Americans were not as open-minded and friendly as she had seen in movies. Instead of complaining, she soon came to the realization that it was only natural that there are friendly and unfriendly people in every country, and she could understand the anti-foreigner sentiments some local people had shown. It was similar to her experiences of seeing her friends in China unaccepting of people from other provinces. For local people to accept international students from China, it may be even more difficult as they had grown up in a totally different environment and have drastically different cultural backgrounds. She did not think it was fair to ask local students to accept international students immediately, especially if they did not have similar interests or hobbies as points of connection. She had trouble making what she called "real friends," meaning that she could go wild or play rough together with them. The American friends she had made during her first year in the United States were merely "friendly," meaning that they could do homework or go out for dinner together and they were quite polite, but there was not much meaningful or in-depth communication among them.

In her assessment, the four years she spent at American high schools were quite challenging and highly rewarding at the same time. It was challenging because there were new hurdles to jump every year as she was making considerable, continuous progress in adapting herself to the new environment. During the first year (her 9th grade, that is), she was prompted to make adjustments both academically and socioculturally, as described above. The reward for her hard work was that she excelled in academic performance. Then, the second year she transferred to the current school which had higher academic standards. In addition to pushing herself harder to meet those standards, she also started doing theater. In order to do better than playing minor roles, she struggled to correct her accent to make herself sound more native. She also had to learn to get along with "theater people," who tended to be quite different from the majority of local students. Although exerting extra pressure and anxiety, the theater experience culminated in the rewarding experience of attending the Edinburg Arts Festival in the summer of her 10th grade where she tried many new things that she had never thought of trying before. She had to reduce her theater activities considerably after entering 11th grade as she started quite a few new things, such as taking AP and IB courses, participating in speech and debate, as well as doing Model United Nations. The academic pressure became so high that during the second semester of her 11th grade she often had to work until late at night, and did not go to bed until 1 or 2 o'clock in the morning. This kind of stressful life continued into the first semester of 12th grade when she had to start preparing college applications.

To a large extent, many of the challenges that made her life stressful were taken on by herself. She acknowledged that at the outset she had participated in many of the activities, such as Model United Nations, out of practical considerations as they would make her resume look good. However, she soon found most of the activities to be interesting and beneficial. Although it was only after a couple of months that she felt much better adjusted, deep in her heart, she never felt at ease. It was this sense of uncertainty and a reasonable level of anxiety that pushed her to work hard. She understood deeply in her heart that one had to exert oneself and make great efforts in order to achieve high and be accomplished, and this was true of all individuals, no matter where they came from and where they were.

The four years of sojourning experiences was transformational for her. Of course, her character and temperament largely remained the same, such as her enterprising spirit. But her way of thinking and values had certainly been transformed. As she described:

> In China nowadays, it is fashionable to do cosmetic surgery and wear expensive clothes. Many of my friends have followed that fashion. If I had stayed in China, I would have probably been the same. I am not saying it is necessarily a bad thing. It is a natural thing for girls to pursue beauty. However, now I may have a different definition of beauty than they do. For example, I would think it is important to have healthy beauty and I would try to make myself more beautiful by doing workout.

Further, she had become more independent and proactive. Since coming to the current school, instead of passively becoming a member of existing ingroups, she had managed to develop a circle of friends which made her feel more at home. She admitted that she did not have any close Chinese friends at the current school, and she seemed to have an easier time making friends with American students than with Chinese students. To her character and temperament played a more important role in developing friendship than cultural backgrounds.

Even though *Rong* seemed to want to transcend cultural barriers and she openly acknowledged that she was not a "political" person, the fact that she came from a totally different environment inevitably affected her adjustment, and she had to learn to deal with those differences. Overall, she felt that the average American did not know much about China; some of them even thought that China was still in the stage where everyone was riding a bicycle to work. Sometimes, the ideological differences were reflected in innocent jokes. For example, a male student in her theater activity often jokingly asked her: "How is our great Chairman Mao doing today," or yell to her things like "go back to your communist country" because somehow he felt it was "cool" to use the word "communist." In 10th grade history class, *Rong* was exposed to more formal and academic discussion on "communism." She could tell that communism was viewed negatively in class, but she did not say anything in class discussion because, according to her: "It is understandable from an American perspective that they do not like communism, and they like their system better… But I don't see why China should not continue the way it is."

When she returned to China in summer after spending one year in America, she realized that she had become different in the eyes of those around her in China. They did not understand why she became unnecessarily polite and kept nodding to people. As she spent more time in America and travelled back and forth between China and America, she noticed more and more changes in herself and found herself to be a stranger in the familiar land of her own country. On the one hand, she became more considerate of others and more compassionate and empathic toward those in need. For example, she would give more money to beggars on the street, and show sincere respect for street artists. On the other hand, she became more critical of and vocal about undesirable and inappropriate behavior. A few months before the interview, she was waiting in a very long line at the airport in China ready to fly back to school in the US. A man went up to her asking if she could let him into the line as he was late for his flight. Her father, who was with her at the time, advised against letting him in, but she let him in because she felt he was in need of help. A few minutes later, another man tried to force into the line without getting permission from anyone or providing any explanation, firmly and politely, she stopped that man from getting into the line. That man even apologized to her.

One factor that contributed to her increased empathy is her increased awareness of some global issues such as poverty and homeless, and what she learned at American schools about the sufferings of all people in other countries. The other factor is that through the sojourning experiences which exposed her to the feeling of restraints, deprivation, and disadvantage, she realized that anyone, including herself, could be in a helpless situation. When in such a situation, one had to be taking a proactive attitude toward those difficulties. As she stated: "When in a disadvantaged situation, you will re-examine yourself and then try to strengthen yourself." The willingness to become more resilient and flexible in making necessary adjustments enabled her to grow and leads to further development and improvement.

Fen: A Case of Separation

Fen was a high school junior when I interviewed him. His height was about average, but overall he was on the thin side. He confirmed during the interview that he did not like the food provided by his host family, which explained his thinness. Similar to *Rong*, *Fen* was quite eloquent and articulate, but in contrast to *Rong*, *Fen* did not demonstrate much composure. In fact, I could feel his restlessness and even anger at times, as well as his need for attention and care. It was clear that he had been struggling adjusting himself to the new environment. During the interview, he repeated three times a line from *Spring and Autumn Annals*, a classical work in ancient China: Those who are not our kin are sure to be of a different heart.

Fen came from a medium-sized city in Northern China, and his parents are private business owners. Neither of his parents went to college, but they were quite successful as business people. In contrast to *Rong* who had to persuade her parents to send her to study overseas, Fen was forced by his parents to start preparing for studying overseas at the age of 13. He described himself as slightly above average in his academic performance before going overseas to study. The reason for his maladjustment may be traced back to the very beginning of the decision-making process regarding whether he would go overseas to study. His parents did not really involve him in making the decision, and instead, it all started when his father attended a lecture at a prestigious university in China where a professor commented how beneficial it would be for children to go overseas to study and how far-sighted of the parents to send their children overseas to study early on. Initially, *Fen* said no to the idea of studying oversea because he did not want to leave his friends and the familiar environment. His mother encouraged him to pursue his dreams overseas, and eventually he reluctantly accepted the idea.

To better prepare himself for studying overseas and especially improve English, *Fen* spent a year in Beijing attending language programs after 8th grade. At the age of 13, he was already living by himself in Beijing looking for rented housing and language programs. It was his estimate that he had spent more than 300,000 Chinese yuan (equivalent of close to $50,000) that year, including rent, living expenses, tuition for language school, and the fees he had paid for study-abroad agencies that helped him with his application.

After one year of preparation in Beijing, he was able to go to a high school in the northeastern part of the United States to be a 9th grader. Before going overseas, he had learned from American movies and rappers that America was a free land where people were friendly, and he had envisioned making friends with local students. Soon after his arrival, he realized that he did not like the new environment. It was a Catholic school which required religion classes, and he could not accept what he was taught in class. Further, he was often made fun of by local students. He had two fights with local students at that school and was suspended for two days the second time because he had hit an American student. Thinking the punishment was unfair since he felt it was the American student who had provoked him first, he refused to have further interactions with local students. In fact, the two fights made him quite unpopular at school, and no American students would even speak to him after the fights. To make things worse, the other six Chinese students who started attending the school around the same time as he did also rubbed him the wrong way. According to *Fen*, those other students were all typical *fuerdai*, or the second-generation scion in a "nouveau riche" family, who would show off their fancy cars and the multiple mansions their family owned. He did not think he was a good student, but he certainly was the best one among them.

Further, *Fen* had serious conflicts with the host family because they would charge his friends who stayed over or did not allow him to use hot water kettle for fear of adding to the electricity bill. There were nights he cried his eyes out with nobody around to comfort him. He lost 40 pounds during his first year in the United States. Feeling like being trapped in a prison, he started looking for schools elsewhere during the second semester and was able to transfer to the current school—with the help of another agent—to attend the 10th grade.

Things got slightly better after the transfer, and he even had something good to say about the school. He liked the GPA system which was based on various components, including multiple assignments and exams. Even though he was not as hostile toward local students after moving to the current school two years ago, he was still reluctant to have much association with them. He felt it was a mistake for his parents to send him overseas. But he could not return to China before completing school because he would be considered a loser by his friends and relatives, and thus his parents would lose face. Further, he owed it to his parents to finish school because of the large sum of money his parents had spent on him. Therefore, he continued to stay and try to finish school even though he felt like living in a prison.

Thinking back, he felt that his parents wanted to send him overseas to study for two reasons. One was that they did it out of practical consideration since they thought that *Fen* would have better job prospects. The other reason was that they had seen many of their friends do so and they were simply trying to keep up with the Joneses. In other words, they wanted to send *Fen* overseas just to satisfy their own vanity. To *Fen*, this was not the right motive, and even though he did not express dissatisfaction openly in the interview, one could feel his resentfulness toward his parents, as demonstrated in the following quote:

> I strongly suggest that those parents who are considering sending their children overseas to do the following things: First, you should know your child well; second, you should try to communicate with your child, and third, do not give too much pressure to your child once they are already overseas… It is not right for any parent who does not spend much time with their child to push their child outside to study overseas hoping that they would somehow become accomplished.

Fen was quite passive in making adjustments, and various factors can explain his maladjustment, such as his distant relationship with his parents and his conflicts with local students at the first school he had attended. Parents' love and support seems to play an important role in students' adjustment, and those who are able to better adjust themselves tend to be those who have a close relationship with their parents. *Fen* seemed to be quite distant from his parents. Even teachers and staff had trouble getting in touch with his parents. Even though there were various factors for his maladjustments, ultimately, it was *Fen*'s refusal to adapt to the new environment that prevented him from adopting a less negative attitude toward the changes he needed to adjust to.

Zhong: In Between Integration and Separation

Zhong struck me as an easy-going and down-to-earth person. Like *Fen*, *Zhong* also came from a medium-sized city in China and business family background. His mother had an associate degree and his father never went to college, but they got pretty wealthy through border trade. He had attended a good public high school before going overseas, but he was frank about his poor academic record when he studied in China and described himself as a student "at the bottom of class" in academic performance. He did not like school, and especially hated drill exercises and exams. As he was muddling along through the 10th grade unhappily, one day his father told him that he would go to the United States to continue his schooling, and that a business partner of his father's who was in the United States would be his guardian. He did not resist this idea as he did not think it would make any difference where to idle away his life. Another option for "at-risk" students like him would have been joining the army where their parents believed they could go through metamorphosis in a cruelly disciplined and demanding—both physically and psychologically—environment. He resisted the idea of joining the military then, but thinking back, he felt "that would not have been such a bad idea," maybe because the road not taken is always tempting, maybe because the road he ended up choosing did not prove to be that easy.

He had his reservations about going overseas to study, among which language concern was the biggest one, and it turned out that his concerns were well justified. He was demoted to the 9th grade when he started school in the United States—after two months of language school, mostly because of his unpreparedness in language. He had to take all English as a Second Language classes during his first semester. He was completely in the dark during the first week, and had no idea what the teacher was saying in class. As a result, he did not do any homework during that week. It took him the whole semester to get accustomed to the English environment at school.

During his first year at the current school there were only five students from China, including himself, but after four years at the time of the interview, there were already over 20 of them, which epitomizes the exponential growth of Chinese students studying in the United States at the secondary level during the past years. To his surprise, he did not feel much homesick mostly because he was able to make some friends quickly, some with Chinese students and some with other international students from Japan and South Korea.

He felt that although he did not learn as much academically as he would have if he had stayed in China for high school, he had learned much more in non-academic aspects. According to him, the subject content in American high school is not as much in-depth. Even for his language skills, although his sense of language had been much improved and he had no problem communicating with others both inside and outside classroom, he felt his vocabulary might have been better had he studied in a Chinese high school. Even after four years at this high school, he still could not fully understand the teachers and other students. He estimated it to be about 70% that he could fully understand for some of the hard subjects such as English and Biology. He was able to understand what was taught and discussed for up to 90% of the time if he could understand the body language and backgrounds of the discussion.

He thoroughly enjoyed the wide range of the curriculum offered at the school, though. For example, he even took a ceramics class, which was unthinkable in a Chinese high school. Like a few other male students from China, *Zhong* expressed the importance of sports for his adaptation. First of all, he became much stronger and physically fit, and it was important to feel healthy physically. Further, playing sports was an important tool for socialization. He was able to make friends, especially with local students, in a natural setting, through playing sports. In fact, it seems to be a repeating theme that sports may help with those

Chinese students' adjustments, especially for male students. More than one male interviewee commented one the importance of sports. Their experiences demonstrated the importance of physical health for students as well as potential socialization function of sports, especially group sports.

Overall, *Zhong*'s adaptation was pretty successful, which was illustrated by his ability to make American friends and his contentment with life. However, he had mixed feelings about the studying-overseas experiences. On the one hand, he felt the experiences he gained during the adaptation process were priceless, and through those social experiences he was able to broaden his horizon and improve his social skills. But on the other hand, for something one wins there is something lost. For example, he regretted that he had gradually lost his friends in China over the past four years. While experiencing drafting away from his old friends in China, he had not developed friendship at such profound levels in his new environment. He used such phrases as "getting stuck" and "being torn apart" to describe that feeling: "When in the US, I do not feel integrated into the society. When going back to China, I feel I cannot keep up with all the changes. It seems that I cannot keep up with either side. It feels like that I am stuck in between. … It is almost like I am split into halves, one half of me is in the US and the other half in China."

Zhong is one of those Chinese students who benefited from studying overseas. For students like *Zhong* who was disengaged in school in China, open to other possibilities, and at the same time mature enough (or at least willing to learn) to take care of himself, the relatively open and flexible education system, as well as its holistic teaching philosophy at American schools may be a better option. In some sense, the opportunity to study overseas saved him. If he had remained in China, he would have been screened out by the competitive test-driven and academically focused system. However, in American school, his interest in school was rekindled and he regained his confidence in life. He was eventually admitted to a 4-year regional public university on the West Coast. Even though this is by no means an impressive accomplishment, it means that he was able to become a self-reliant, contributing member of society who is able to find his own happiness in life, which is probably better than the possible alternative outcome if he had remained in China.

Concluding Remarks

During the process of adaptation, there is potential for students' knowledge to be enhanced about themselves and other cultures as also their understanding of the common predicament and vulnerability of humanity. There is also potential for such parachute kids to hone their skills in thinking, analyzing, and performing tasks, and potential for cultivating the values of open-mindedness, empathy, compassion, and respect for diversity and difference. As a result, these students could be potentially better equipped for the challenges and hardships during the process of adaptation.

Of course, the growth does not happen automatically through international travelling and sojourning. As Caruana (2014) states: "Encountering otherness abroad may involve rejection or narrow selection rather than openness, since the 'surrender' to openness is situational and dependent on the nature of intercultural contact" (p. 90). Only those students who learn, through their international sojourning experience, that anyone could be in a helpless and disadvantaged situation, and that those who can turn the experience of disadvantage into an opportunity for re-examining and strengthening themselves, will be able to realize this potential.

References

Adler, P. S. (1975). The transitional experience: An alternative view of culture shock. *Journal of Humanistic Psychology, 15*, 13–23.

Berry, J. W. (1974). Psychological aspects of cultural pluralism: Unity and identity reconsidered. *Topics in Culture Learning, 2*, 17–22.

Berry, J. W. (1997). Immigration, acculturation and adaptation. *Applied Psychology, 46*, 5–68.

Berry, J. W., Phinney, J. S., Sam, D. L., & Vedder, P. (2006). Immigrant youth: Acculturation, identity, and adaptation. *Applied Psychology: An International Review, 55*(3), 303–332.

Bock, P. K. (1970). *Culture shock*. Lanham, MD: University Press of America.

Brown, H. D. (1980). The optimal distance model of second language acquisition. *TESOL Quarterly, 14*, 157–164.

Caruana, V. (2014). Re-thinking global citizenship in higher education: From cosmopolitanism and international mobility to cosmopolitanisation, resilience and resilient thinking. *Higher Education Quarterly, 68*(1), 85–104.

Cheng, B. (2019). Sociocultural adaptation of "parachute kids" from mainland China. *British Journal of Guidance & Counselling*, 1–18, https://doi.org/10.1080/03069885.2019.1643006

Furnham, A. (1995). Psychological and socio-cultural variables as predictors of adjustment in cross-cultural transitions. *Psychologia, 38*, 238–251.

Garza-Guerrero, A. C. (1974). Culture shock: Its mourning and the vicissitudes of identity. *Journal of the American Psychoanalytic Association, 22*, 408–429.

Gordon, M. (1964). *Assimilation in American life*. New York: Oxford University Press.

Gullahourn, J. T., & Gullahorn, J. E. (1960). The role of the academic man as a cross-cultural mediator. *American Sociological Review, 25*(3), 414–417.

Kim, Y. (1988). *Communication and cross-cultural adaptation*. Clevedon: Multilingual Matters.

Lysgaard, S. (1955). Adjustment in a foreign society: Norwegian Fulbright grantees visiting the United States. *International Social Science Bulletin, 7*, 45–51.

Oberg, K. (1960). Culture shock: Adjustment to new cultural environments. *Practical Anthropology, 7*, 177–182.

Phinney, J. S. (1990). Ethnic identity in adolescents and adults: A review of research. *Psychological Bulletin, 108*, 499–514.

Redfield, R., Linton, R., & Herskovits, M. (1936). Memorandum on the study of acculturation. *American Anthropologist, 38*, 149–152.

Searle, W., & Ward, C. (1990). The prediction of psychological antd sociocultural adjustment during cross-cultural transitions. *International Journal of Intercultural Relations, 14*, 449–464.

Tsong, Y., & Liu, Y. (2008). Parachute kids and astronaut families. In N. Tewari & A. N. Alvarez (Eds.), *Asian American psychology: Current perspectives* (pp. 365–379). New York, NY: Psychology Press.

Ward, C., & Kennedy, A. (1993). Psychological and socio-cultural adjustment during cross-cultural transitions: A comparison of secondary students overseas and at home. *International Journal of Psychology, 28*(2), 129–147.

Chapter 8
The Role of Chinese Supplemental Education Service Organizations in the International Mobility of Chinese Students

Introduction

If you walk the streets of Beijing's Haidian District, where many Chinese high-tech firms such as Lenovo and Baidu have located their headquarters, you will see prominently displayed in subway stations and supermarkets the eye-catching posters advertising Chinese supplemental education service (SES) organizations.[1] The messages these organizations promote—how many of their students were admitted to Harvard and Yale last year; their students' average TOEFL and SAT scores; their teams of international consultants—make it easy to see the role of SES organizations in the ever-growing waves of Chinese students studying abroad.

This chapter investigates this often-overlooked player in international student mobility: SES organizations and the industry they form. China's SES industry is the world's largest and fastest growing of its kind. Non-existent before the 1980s, its total annual revenue surpassed 200 billion USD in 2015 (Deloitte China, 2018). Each year the SES industry recruits nearly one-tenth of China's enormous population into its classrooms (KPMG, 2011). For some leading SES organizations, such as Supernova and United IELTS,[2] revenue from their overseas-studies-oriented test-preparation classes (e.g., TOEFL, GRE, and SAT classes) comprises more than one-third of their total revenue (e.g., Lu, 2002).

---

[1] The SES sector provides various non-degree-oriented educational services, such as test-preparation, foreign language training, and after-school tutoring. In this chapter, I also include educational consulting and broker agencies in the SES industry.

[2] All SES brand names here are pseudonyms. Using pseudonyms helps protect the identities of my interviewees. In a chapter that is based on non-random cases and their historical events, complete anonymity is indeed impossible. Using pseudonyms, however, creates a buffer for my informants. To make the names consistent throughout the chapter, I had to change a few book and article titles in the reference when real names of organizations and people are included in the original titles.

© Springer Nature Singapore Pte Ltd. 2020
B. Cheng et al., *The New Journey to the West*, Education in the Asia-Pacific Region: Issues, Concerns and Prospects 53, https://doi.org/10.1007/978-981-15-5588-6_8

To assess the roles of SES organizations in overseas education for Chinese students, I first introduce the social context for the emergence of these organizations. After demonstrating the shift of SES organization strategies over time, this chapter highlights how multiple niche markets, such as TOEFL, GRE, and SAT, have evolved and formed an integrated industry. A discussion of how these test-preparation schools helped Chinese students acquire indispensable information to crack the tests and apply for overseas colleges follows. I further show the ways in which test-preparation schools instilled in students the meaning and value of study-abroad and increased demand for overseas studies. The implications of my findings for rethinking the push–pull model conclude the chapter.

Context and the Chronology

Let me start with the shifting contexts and the chronology of SES industry's development. Because of language, information, and cultural barriers associated with overseas studies, participation in preparatory schools was not uncommon among Chinese students who studied abroad before 1980. Even communist leaders, such as Deng Xiaoping, attended preparatory schools before their overseas studies in Europe (Vogel, 2013). This section focuses on what happened after the early 1980s when Deng's social and economic reforms began. There are two distinct stages in the SES industry's development: the first spans the 1980s and 1990s, and the second involves the post-2000 years. The following sections introduce the social contexts of the two stages and elaborate on the changing landscapes of the industry during these two stages.

The First Stage

Beginning in the late 1970s, Chinese leaders pushed toward modernization of China partly by learning from the West and sending students to the United States. As a result, most Chinese students who studied abroad in the late 1970s and early 1980s were on a state-sponsored model (Orleans, 1988). They often had to sign political affidavits to guarantee returning to China after their overseas studies. Under this state-sponsored model, the state played an integral role in deciding who would be rewarded with the opportunity to study abroad. US universities also relied upon the Chinese state's recommendations. Even when a language test was required, most often the Chinese state designed and administered the test. There was no need to take or prepare for standardized tests such as TOEFL or GRE (Qian, 1996, pp. 35–40).

Conditions began to change in the mid-1980s when overseas studies in the United States became fashionable among Chinese students, resulting in an explosion of the self-sponsored model. From 1980 to 1986, the annual number of overseas Chinese students increased by a factor of 20 (Institute of International

Education, 1980–1990). The vast majority of overseas students then were graduate students from elite universities, such as Peking and Tsinghua University. Living in an era when China's new market economy had just begun expanding, even these elite students could not afford the tuition of US colleges, and students often had to apply for financial aid from these colleges (Zhao, 2001, p. 135). As the self-sponsored model gained popularity, applications for admission and financial aid became more competitive. Chinese students increasingly viewed high TOEFL and GRE scores as determining factors for securing financial aid. In the late 1980s, the Tiananmen Student Movement provided another boost for overseas studies and test-preparation. Students rushed to participate in TOEFL and GRE tests because they were worried about China's future and feared that the studying-abroad gate might be closed again.

These factors combined to create a soaring demand for high scores in TOEFL and GRE. As a result, test-preparation SES schools mushroomed. Early market leaders were affiliated with state universities and they were led by professors from these universities. Clear examples were SES organizations affiliated with Peking University and Beijing Foreign Languages Institute (currently Beijing Foreign Studies University). The vast majority of SES teachers were English instructors in these state universities. These teachers worked part-time in TOEFL/GRE schools to earn extra money.

Despite the early domination of state-affiliated schools, market leaders soon shifted to a new group—SES organizations led by entrepreneurs who either had no higher education experience or had held only marginal positions in the state education system. For example, the Big Four SES organizations in Beijing's TOEFL/GRE market in the late 1980s were Seven Swords, Cornerstone, Supernova, and Pioneers. While the founders of the last two schools were lecturers of English in state universities, the entrepreneurs of the first two schools had not had any college experience. Entrepreneurs of this new group soon realized that they did not have to replicate the way state universities taught English. They were also eager to reduce the bargaining power of state university-affiliated teachers. These teachers committed to SES jobs half-heartedly but considered themselves the key to attracting students. Entrepreneurs began hiring younger lecturers of English and later even tapped lecturers and gradu-ate students of other majors. In the 1990s, some of the leading SES schools even hired high school dropouts and street vendors as their GRE teachers.

The 1990s witnessed intense competition among SES schools and the rise of Supernova. Leading SES schools in TOEFL and GRE were concentrated in Beijing's Haidian District, where more than 30 universities were located. These SES organi-zations rented shabby classrooms from state education institutions and provided few services beyond teaching to the tests. Because TOEFL/GRE customers were concentrated in Haidian, leading SES organizations could combine large class sizes with cheap tuition.[3] The dense population of students in this district, on the other hand, meant that SES schools would inevitably cannibalize each other. Supernova

---

[3] In 2000, for example, Supernova had total revenue of 100 million RMB and recruited 150,000 students. That means each student only paid about 666 RMB (less than 100 USD in 2000).

had wiped out the other three leading brands by the end of the 1990s. In 2000, Supernova enrolled 150,000 students, which means that it serviced and profited from 80% of Beijing's and 50% of the entire nation's TOEFL/GRE market (Pang, 2004). During its competition with other brands, Supernova's cheap tuition and free information sessions played an integral role in its success. The biggest contributor to Supernova's domination, however, was its mass teaching model.

Mass teaching is a model that combines large class size, competitive salaries, young and eloquent teachers, competition among teachers, and performance-based teacher evaluations. Supernova was a pioneer in transforming its teaching force from university instructors to eloquent youth who excelled in speaking in front of large audiences. Supernova teachers were forced to compete against each other for student evaluations in the same class, and students' impression-based evaluations were the sole determinant of teacher performance ratings. In order to achieve superior evaluations, teachers had to compete with each other not only on delivery of test-preparation skills but also in recitation of self-help stories, nationalist jokes, and even in singing and dancing. Such a performative teaching style proved effective in attracting students. Students found Supernova teachers so "passionate," "funny," and "patriotic" that they couldn't wait to share their class experiences and favorite teacher quotes with friends and classmates (Supernova Archive No. 10; Lu, 2002; Interviews with multiple Supernova teachers and students in April 2014 and May 2015). This explains how Supernova could recruit thousands of students from all over China in 1999 when it was only operating in Beijing. However successful Supernova was during the 1990s, it was a local specialist focused on two tests, rather than a generalist company with multiple product lines.

Despite ample evidence documenting the large number of high-scoring students produced by Supernova, there is no systematic data supporting the effectiveness of its pedagogy. As I mentioned earlier, Supernova evaluated teachers based on student impressions rather than student educational gains. There was an absence of pre-test and post-test data. Little information was gathered to accurately assess the degree of student improvement. To compound the problem, a large proportion of Supernova's students in the 1980s and 1990s were students from elite universities. As a result, there was no way to ascertain the added value of Supernova classes for these already high-achievers.

The Second Stage

The landscape of the SES industry altered after 2000 in response to several macro and structural changes.

One of these macro changes was China's deeper engagement with the global economy. In 2002, China entered the World Trade Organization and became the world's manufacturing center. This helped sustain China's economic growth and fueled the rise of the middle-, upper-middle, and elite classes in China. Parents from these globally minded economic classes were eager to send their children to other countries. These parents could afford higher tuition and wanted their children exposed to Western culture at younger ages.

Another macro change was the rising popularity of Britain, Australia, and other Commonwealth nations as host countries for Chinese students. These countries were ideal destinations for middle-class families because higher education in these countries was more accessible through a self-financed model, and it cost less time and tuition than did US higher education. After the terrorist attack on 9/11 and the added restrictions on US visas, Chinese students found the British Commonwealth countries even more appealing.

In concert with these changes, SES organizations and the entire industry underwent a transition. First, the 2000s witnessed the emergence of new niche markets targeting young Chinese students and those who were interested in Commonwealth countries. The most notable niche markets included SES organizations focusing on the IELTS and SAT. For example, there were only 20,000 Chinese students who took the IELTS in 2000, but this number increased to 350,000 in 2010 (China Education Online, 2011). While there were fewer IELTS takers than TOEFL takers in 2000, by 2010 the number of IELTS takers was twice as large as that of TOEFL takers (China Education Online, 2011). As for the SAT exam, the number of test-takers increased from 1000 in 2006 to 30,000 in 2010, an exponential growth in only 4 years (China Education Online, 2011).

Another noticeable evolution was the popularity of small-sized classes. As I mentioned earlier, while the primary customers before 2000 were academic elites aiming at US graduate schools, customers after 2000 came from economically better-off families who were increasingly interested in undergraduate degrees and high school diplomas in the United States and British Commonwealth countries. The increase in the numbers of young students also increased parental involvement in the SES classes. Parents did not mind paying higher tuition for small-sized classes and preferred educational gains in test scores to entertaining teachers. Mass teaching was in decline and small-sized classes became the new fashion. To help students boost their test scores, SES organizations not only changed their teacher evaluation rubrics to place stronger emphasis on educational gains, but they also hired and trained supervisors whose job was to monitor students' progress.

The formation of new market niches was accompanied by the rise of new market leaders. For example, United IELTS was founded in 2000 as a school specializing in IELTS test-preparation, and it had developed into a national chain with more than 60% market share in IELTS by 2010. In the meantime, Supernova, the former specialist in TOEFL/GRE also expanded to IELTS and SAT and occupied sizable market shares in these niches. Drawing on its massive student pool, Supernova also strengthened its overseas-study-oriented consulting and broker businesses. By the mid-2000s, Supernova had evolved into the largest SES organization in China. In 2006, it became the first Chinese SES firm that launched on an overseas stock market (New York Stock Exchange). In 2010, United IELTS was also listed on the US stock market.

The IPOs of Supernova and United IELTS subjected these organizations to the influence of worldwide financial markets. Global investors realized that sending

Chinese students overseas was a lucrative business, and investments poured in. While SES organizations were once non-capital-intensive, now SES organizations started securing investments from venture capitalists. Some SES organizations even engaged in mergers and acquisitions of other or foreign SES organizations. For example, there have been two SES organizations that had enjoyed exponential growth in a short time and listed themselves in the US stock markets solely by acquiring other Chinese SES companies, including a number of companies that specialized in SAT and TOEFL.

In the 2010s, some leading SES organizations have adopted a new strategy—internationalization. These leading SES organizations are no longer content with sending Chinese students overseas. They have begun to provide services to their former students who now live and study in the United States and other countries. One example is Lingua Fun, a leading TOEFL and SAT provider in Eastern China. This company now operates an office in New York City whose job is to help Chinese students in US secondary schools polish college application essays as well as to design extracurricular activities for these students. To purchase a full package of services that help a student from middle school to college entrance, a family must pay over 100,000 USD (Interview with a Lingua Fun manager in June 2019). Operating in New York City not only allows Lingua Fun to stay close to their customers and US higher education institutions, but also enables this company to take advantage of the stagnant wages of the US workforce. Although a large proportion of this company's consultants graduated from elite colleges such as Columbia University and New York University, their salary is not significantly higher than that of employees with commensurate education background in China (China Education Online, 2011). In addition to establishing overseas offices, SES organizations also internationalize themselves by undertaking short-term global trips. Trident Education, a Guangzhou-based test-preparation and educational consulting firm, regularly organizes their students to fly to the United States and take the SAT test.[4]

The Roles of SES Organizations in Overseas Studies

This section discusses the various roles SES organizations play in Chinese students' studying-abroad process. The study-abroad process in China encompasses making decisions to study abroad as well as actually preparing for and taking tests and executing the application. I will show that SES organizations not only play supportive roles in this process but also act as the "visible hand" in creating ever-larger waves of Chinese nationals studying abroad.[5]

---

[4] There are two reasons why Chinese students travel abroad to take SAT tests. First, there is no SAT test center in Mainland China at this time; as a result, Chinese students have to at least travel to Hong Kong to take the test. Second, There is an unproven assertion among some Chinese students that SAT tests in the United States are easier than those in Hong Kong.

[5] According to neoclassic economics, demand and supply in a market function like "the invisible hand." Studies of international student mobility also employ the demand and supply framework

Supportive Role

It is clear that SES organizations play a supportive role in facilitating the studying-abroad process: SES organizations provide students and their families with test-preparation assistance and application information *after* these clients have made up their minds to engage in overseas studies.

Test-preparation classes offered by SES organizations cover a variety of test-taking-related aspects. First, these services help decode the patterns of tests. SES organizations espouse the philosophy of teaching to the test. Teachers of these organizations analyze past materials to find out the pattern of a test. For example, Supernova's GRE Vocabulary, one of its best-selling books and also known to Chinese students as the Red Bible, was based on systematic analyses of the frequency of GRE words in previous tests.

Test-preparation classes also cover the language foundation of tests. TOEFL and GRE classes, for example, familiarize Chinese students with certain vocabulary these students did not have a chance to learn in their English classes. In a book on TOEFL listening, for example, the author—a Supernova teacher—introduced a number of idiomatic expressions and slang words commonly used in American English. Similarly, GRE classes equip Chinese students with academic vocabulary.

SES organization classes sometimes convey a contradictory message—the uselessness of the language foundation of tests. Teachers send this message either to convince students without a solid language background to join the cause of overseas studies, or to show the "magic effect" of following teachers' test-cracking skills. In fact, a few teachers at Supernova became nationally renowned because they claimed students could conquer TOEFL listening and reading without understanding much English. In published books and class recordings, for example, Supernova teachers inform students there is a pattern in the old TOEFL listening section—whenever you hear about apple pie, the answer is always "delicious" (e.g., Wu, 1998).

The third major supportive role SES organizations play involves closing the information and cultural gap in the application process for Chinese applicants. The application and admission processes of US colleges differ significantly from those in the Chinese system, which is solely based on test scores. For Chinese applicants, writing application essays and asking professors to prepare recommendation letters not only entail acquiring an exotic set of functional skills but also requires overcoming cultural barriers. One such barrier is that professors in Chinese universities, especially those who did not attend US colleges, were neither familiar with the idea of recommendation letters nor proficient in English. The lack of exposure to information and culture regarding US college applications was most severe for students who came from non-elite colleges and therefore lacked alumni networks for information and cultural tool-kits.

(e.g., Findlay, 2011). However, Chandler (1993) illustrates that the economic structure in the United States has evolved into an era that is dominated by large bureaucratic corporations. These large corporations play such an important role in the economy that they are like "the visible hand" of the market.

Test-preparation SES organizations became the venue where Chinese students could close those gaps. In the 1990s, TOEFL and GRE schools in Beijing regularly held free information sessions about how to apply for admissions and financial aid of US universities. Supernova, for example, used free information sessions as a powerful marketing tool to attract students and promote its teachers and brand. Supernova even opened a library that hosted a large collection of US university application-related books.

While elite students before 2000 usually handled the actual application by themselves, after 2000 students and their parents significantly increased their use of consulting and brokering organizations. The direct participation of these organizations in essay writing and recommendation letters raises the issue of cheating. Indeed, cheating and scams exist. In some cases, these organizations cheated students by recommending unaccredited colleges that paid these organizations fees comprising 20–30% of a referred client's first-year tuition. In some other cases, these organizations cheated overseas colleges by inventing attractive stories for the application essay and fabricating recommendation letters. Still other organizations printed inflated admissions statistics in their advertisements to attract students.

As Chinese consumers became more quality-sensitive and as the competition among consulting-oriented SES firms intensified, those that relied solely on cheating have lost their steam. New market leaders increasingly highlight hiring former admission officers and graduates of elite US colleges as their consultants. The "cultural capital" of these people in the application process—the firm grasp of the meaning, rituals, and tacit knowledge required for every step of the admissions process—constitutes new weapons in the fierce market competition. Consequently, consulting-oriented SES firms have also evolved into a top industry that employs Chinese study-abroad returnees.

Beyond Supportive Roles

SES organizations also move beyond their supportive roles. In contrast to the conventional wisdom that SES organizations do not become relevant until students and parents have made up their mind to study overseas, Chinese SES organizations play an active role during and even before the decision-making process begins.

Chinese SES organizations act as the "visible hand" behind the ever-growing waves of Chinese students studying overseas (Lin, 2020). In a nutshell, market leaders such as Supernova not only provided information and test-preparation training, but they also instilled in students the meaning of studying-abroad and test-preparation processes. These organizations adopted a variety of "framing strategies" to convince students why they should study abroad, creating demand and facilitating decisions for overseas studies.[6]

The first distinct framing strategy, most notable in Supernova TOEFL/GRE classes before 2000, entails using self-help discourses. Instead of depicting overseas studies as a means to achieve other goals, such a framing strategy positions studying abroad as an end in itself: to study abroad means going beyond one's self and making one's life complete. The account below by a Supernova student captures the essence of this framing strategy:

> In the eyes of Supernova teachers, US is a place we should and must go. In every ceremony and class, Supernova teachers passionately called upon us to conquer the US. It seems to them that our Chinese students are born for the US.... According to Supernova, studying abroad is not a means, but an end. If you can study abroad, you are a winner; otherwise you are a loser. In this massive wave for studying-abroad, we should not belittle the role of Supernova. I do not know if we have thought about what we would do after we go out. Probably we study abroad simply for the sake of studying abroad. (Lu, 2002, p. 112)

Supernova teachers also applied this framing strategy to the test-preparation process. For example, some Supernova teachers mentioned that memorizing GRE vocabulary entailed enduring tremendous hardship and these words were not useful in real lives. According to these teachers, however, undergoing such hardship and working on trivial matters are exactly how a student perfects oneself.

Another salient framing strategy used by Supernova before 2000 involved adopting a nationalist discourse. This strategy depicted studying abroad as an opportunity for students to learn from the West first and build a stronger China after returning from the West. For example, Supernova teachers called upon students to study abroad early and come back sooner. Supernova also labeled itself as "the bridge for Chinese students to study abroad and the rainbow connecting them back to China" (Supernova Archive No. 2, p. 2). These strategies not only earned Supernova teachers the reputation of being patriots but also reduced various political risks, such as being criticized for inducing a brain drain.

These framing strategies not only contributed to the popularity of Supernova among students but also made students more determined to study overseas. Because Supernova teachers competed with each other for evaluations from students, these teachers spent a substantial proportion of their class time on framing and on stories that were not directly related to TOEFL/GRE tests. Students found these performative approaches lively and refreshing. Through word-of-mouth advertising, a large number of students from all over China began to come to Beijing to attend Supernova classes. According to informal surveys conducted by two Supernova teachers during 1996–1997, usually 30%–50% students in their classes had not yet developed a clear agenda for studying abroad (Interviews with two Supernova teachers in April and May 2014). Many students chose to attend TOEFL/GRE classes because many of their friends were attending and because they had heard legendary stories about Supernova teachers. In the year 2000, Supernova, still primarily a TOEFL/GRE

---

[6] Framing, according to Goffman (1974), is "schemata of interpretation" that enables individuals to "perceive, identify and label" (Goffman, 1974), rendering events and occurrences meaningful.

school, recruited 150,000 students. In comparison, the total number of TOEFL and GRE test-takers in China was only estimated to be about 120,000. In other words, there were more Chinese students who attended Supernova's TOEFL/GRE classes than those who took the test. A large number of Supernova students did not aim at taking these tests. Many students participated in Supernova classes as undecided students. But there is evidence documenting how some of these students became more determined to engage in overseas studies after they attended Supernova (Supernova Archives No. 2, No. 10). Supernova teachers' framing strategies catalyzed this transition.

After 2000, new market leaders, especially those in SAT and IELTS niches, adopted a different framing strategy, one in which they used family-improvement discourses. As I mentioned earlier, the new trends after 2000 include the rise of small-sized classes, a higher percentage of self-sponsored and self-financed students and greater involvement from parents of economically better-off families. In light of these changes, new market leaders started framing studying abroad as an opportunity for family improvement—the entire family could immigrate to Western countries and raise their status to that of the global elites. Such a framing strategy captured the heart of Chinese upper-middle and elite families who were anxious about becoming global elites and concerned about losing their class status during China's rapid social change. The popularity of this new framing strategy does not mean self-help or nationalist discourses disappeared. Distinct discourses appeal to different groups of people. These different framing strategies have been co-existing to maintain the vitality of the study-abroad movement.

Since the mid-2010s, a new framing strategy has surfaced. This is a new era of anti-globalization. Around the world we are witnessing the triumph of populist leaders who blame immigrants and evoke racist discourses. Such an environment has led to confusion and fear among many potential overseas students from China: is it still safe to study in another country? Are we still welcome as we were in the past? Chinese SES organizations have adopted the new role of appeasing Chinese parents and students. For example, Ivy Gate, an SES consulting firm specializing in sending Chinese students to US Ivy League colleges, published a blog article claiming "nothing to be worried about studying abroad in the US. US Consulate and President Trump have both mentioned there is no change to the US visa policy. We hope you can rebuild your confidence in studying in the US. Rest assured" (Ivy Gate Archive, No. 1).

Concluding Remarks

This section discusses the implications of my findings about the supportive and more active roles played by SES organizations in overseas studies. I start with the issues of fairness and inequality for Chinese applicants and conclude with the policy and theoretical implications for Chinese students, families, and society.

Because cheating and scams are sometimes involved, the penetration of SES organizations in the application process can damage the fairness of this process. In addition to the above-mentioned frauds in the consulting and brokering services, test-preparation classes can also induce unfairness. In some extreme cases, SES organizations send their teachers to take the test on behalf of a student test-taker. In many other cases, unfairness can take a more hidden form. For example, some GMAT teachers regularly take the tests themselves so they can have a firm grasp of the test prompts and share these prompts with students (Interview with a GMAT teacher in April 2014). When cheating and scams occur, Chinese students who follow the rules risk losing their competitiveness. To colleges in the United States and other host countries, the loss of fairness implies that they are not admitting ideal students.

Cheating and scams also raise the concern of fairness between nations. If a large number of Chinese students employ problematic services offered by SES while most students in another country do not, should we claim that Chinese students are enjoying an unfair advantage? A case during the early 2000s suggests that things can be more complicated than they seem. In 2001, the US-based Educational Testing Service (ETS)—the designer and administrator of TOEFL and GRE—sent a letter to a large number of US colleges, warning of Chinese students' "unfair advantages" due to the provision of pirated test materials by some Chinese SES organizations. Consequently, the GRE tests in China switched from a computer-based format to a paper-format.

Using pirated test materials or using them without permission from test administrators took place against two backdrops: first, before 2000 there was no legitimate channel through which Chinese students could obtain test materials (Lu, 2002); second, neither the idea of intellectual property nor any laws related to intellectual property existed at that time in China. More importantly, there were factors other than SES organizations contributing to the unusually high average GRE scores by Chinese test-takers. Due to the rise of the Internet as an information-sharing platform, the vast number of Chinese test-takers and the limited volume of the test bank, Chinese students could drain all test prompts in a short period of time and share them with other students. As a result, potential test takers could easily know the prompts in advance. Within some Chinese Internet communities in the early 2000s, students even encouraged fellow Chinese students to reciprocate the favor by sharing test prompts because South Korean and Indian students were allegedly doing the same thing. Certainly, sharing such information violated ETS rules as well as a series of moral codes. What many observers often neglect to consider, however, is a deeper cultural difference: while Chinese students often take it for granted that one should decode test patterns and spend ample time on preparing for tests (Lu, 2002), the ideas of "teaching to the test" and "studying to the test" are highly controversial in the United States and other Western countries (e.g., Popham, 2001; Volante, 2004). In short, this case demonstrates the damage to fairness caused by SES organizations, but it also warns against oversimplifying their negative roles based on ethnocentric views.

Even if there is no cheating or fraud, the fact that SES organizations increasingly charge high tuition and lean toward elite classes raises the issue of inequality. Some SES organizations are not shy about targeting elite-class people as their primary customers. The founder of Lingua Fun, for example, mentioned that their vision was to become Audi or BMW in the SES market because "there were over 2 million Chinese families that own at least 30 million USD investable income, and we only need 5% of this market to be successful" (Interview with the founder of Lingua Fun in June 2019). What will happen down the road if this trend continues, however, is that overseas colleges and universities will increasingly see polished essays and nicely orchestrated extracurricular activities of students from wealthy Chinese families.

Existing literature rarely considers SES organizations as a transnational pheonomenon. It seems to concern only policy-makers of the country where SES organizations are located. However, my findings indicate that even domestically operating SES organizations can exert a tremendous impact on foreign higher education sectors. It is imperative for policy makers to consider transnational cooperation in order to regulate SES organizations more effectively.

It is also essential for Chinese policy makers to regulate SES organizations with more realistic policies. From the 1980s to 2000s, SES organizations in China were supervised by local Education Bureaus as non-private and not-for-profit educational entities. These entities were not allowed to register as corporations and could not list themselves on domestic stock markets. These policies were not only difficult to implement but also so unrealistic that they encouraged entrepreneurs to circumvent these policies. For example, Haidian's Education Bureau made it clear that the founders of TOEFL/GRE schools had to be professors from state universities at the associate level or above. Such an unrealistic and mechanical policy excluded otherwise capable and compliant entrepreneurs. Eventually, only retired professors who were qualified and others who dared to circumvent the requirements became entrepreneurs in this industry. In the late 2010s, the Ministry of Education implemented new unrealistic policies when it mandated that all SES teachers be licensed and SES organizations use classrooms that provide each student at least three square meters. These policies were symbolic as well as biased in favor of large organizations.

In a sense, poor policies reflect the limited options of Chinese regulators and their lack of enforcement capabilities. For example, officials in the Education Bureau have complained that they know little about what TOEFL and GRE tests are for; therefore, there is nothing they can do to regulate the educational content of SES organizations. In light of this lack of effective regulation on Chinese SES organizations, there are several strategies education institutions in the United States and other destination countries could adopt. First, these institutions can increase the direct contact with Chinese students, as well as enhance the availability and transparency of their information. As some US universities have already done, faculty members on admission committees can add an extra round of interviews to test Chinese students for English language proficiency. Another strategy is to enforce rule compliance by cooperating with leading Chinese SES organizations. For example, ETS has already established strategic partnerships with some leading Chinese SES organizations. This not only helps disseminate authentic test materials but it also provides a catalyst for the institutionalization of these SES organizations.

My third suggestion for overseas higher educational institutions that recruit a large number of Chinese students is to familiarize themselves with practices of Chinese SES organizations. Some higher education institutions' recent moves, such as abolishing SAT scores in undergraduate admissions, may help dampen the impact of SES organizations. But such moves, when not paralleled with knowledge about how SES organizations operate, might lead to greater influence of SES organizations that focus on polishing essays rather than on preparing for admissions tests.

The fact that SES organizations play such a significant role in overseas studies also prompts us to rethink the push-pull framework. In previous chapters, we have demonstrated the validity of this framework. Despite its apparent merits, the push–pull approach to overseas studies assumes that students' motivations and the demand to study abroad are natural and intrinsic, or merely responses to state-level changes. Rarely do studies theorize student motivation as social constructs that can be created and manipulated by external players, such as SES organizations. In this chapter, I have shown that SES organizations can use framing strategies to instill meaning in overseas studies, thus creating demand and motivation. I have also elucidated how SES organizations interpret current political atmospheres for students. In other words, these organizations might not be able to change the actual push or pull factors, but they can exert a huge impact on how students perceive push and pull factors. Push–pull factors are not necessarily independent from student motivations as many studies suggest. Rather, they are intertwined and the ways in which they interact depend to a certain degree upon organizations that interpret push and pull factors.

This chapter also urges us to rethink the studying-abroad process as a one-time decision-making event. Indeed, it appears entirely legitimate to consider an individual family's decision to study abroad as a rational choice. By rational, I mean that stakeholders have weighed costs and benefits carefully and have outlined clear goals and specific plans before implementing their decision. What I have revealed about SES organizations reminds us of a more complicated and contingent process: many students experiment on a variety of options, such as attending TOEFL/GRE schools, to determine their fitness with overseas studies before thinking through the costs and benefits. It is often through, instead of before, these experiments that the decisions for overseas studies are made. This is not only because attending these schools equips students with more information about overseas studies, but also because such experimental processes allow students to build a peer community and even create social fads.

References

Chandler, A. (1993). *The visible hand: The managerial revolution in American business.* Cambridge, MA: Belknap Press.

China Education Online. (2011). *Reports on the trend of studying abroad.* Retrieved from http://liuxue.eol.cn/html/lxrep/ (www.eol.cn)

Deloitte China. (2018). *A new era of education: China education development report.* Beijing: Deloitte China.

Findlay, A. M. (2011). An assessment of supply and demand-side theorizations of international student mobility. *International Migration, 49*(2), 162–190.

Goffman, E. (1974). *Frame analysis: An essay on the organization of experience.* Cambridge: Harvard University Press.

Institute of International Education. (1980–1990). *Open doors: Report on international educational exchange.* New York: IIE.

Ivy Gate Archive No. 1

KPMG. (2011). *Education industry in China.* Hong Kong: KPMG Partner Firm.

Lin, L. (2020). The visible hand behind study-abroad waves: Cram schools, organizational framing and the international mobility of Chinese students. *Higher Education, 79*(2), 259–274.

Lu, Y. (2002). *Oriental carriage: The legends from Peking University to Supernova.* Beijing: Guangming Daily Press.

Orleans, L. A. (1988). *Chinese students in America: Policies, issues, and numbers.* Washington, DC: National Academy Press.

Pang, R. (2004, November 12). After friends vied each others and senior officers established their own businesses, Su had to steer Supernova by himself. *Southern Weekends.*

Popham, W. J. (2001). Teaching to the test. *Educational Leadership, 58*(6), 16–20.

Qian, N. (1996). *Studying in U.S.A: The stories of an era.* Nanjing: Jiangsu Liberal Arts Press.

Supernova Archives No. 1–10.

Vogel, E. (2013). *Deng Xiaoping and the Transformation of China.* Belknap Press.

Volante, L. (2004). Teaching to the test: What every educator and policy-maker should know. *Canadian Journal of Educational Administration and Policy.* Issue 35.

Wu, L. (1998). *The undertone of the TOEFL listening test.* Beijing: World Knowledge Press.

Zhao, D. (2001). *The power of Tiananmen: State-society relations and the 1989 Beijing student movement.* Chicago: University of Chicago Press.

Chapter 9
Re-examining the Concept of Chinese Learner: Cultivating a Cosmopolitan Spirit Through International Sojourning

Introduction

As illustrated in previous chapters, international students may face difficulties that are caused by cultural, social, economic, and political differences, and that Chinese students might encounter even more challenges than other international students due to the larger differences between China and the United States in their cultural environment and educational system. *Jiang Xueqin*, a curriculum director in two prestigious public high schools in Beijing, who has had rich experience working in and studying Chinese education, thinks that even graduates of his schools who are considered among the brightest in the country "have struggled to adapt to the Western classroom as much as their peers from less elite schools" (Jiang, 2011). Research has recorded various challenges faced by Chinese students studying in North American (i.e., American and Canadian) colleges and universities (Huang & Klinger, 2006; Myles, Qian, & Cheng, 2002). The *Chronicle of Higher Education* tells such a story (Bartlett & Fischer, 2011):

> Last fall, Kent E. St. Pierre [at the University of Delaware] was teaching an intermediate accounting class with 35 students, 17 of them from China. Within a couple of weeks, all but three of the non-Chinese students had dropped the course. Why did the American students flee? "They said the class was very quiet," recalls Mr. St. Pierre, who considers himself a 1960s-style liberal and says he's all for on-campus diversity. But, he agrees, "it was pretty deadly."

This story vividly illustrates the kind of difficulties faced by Chinese students studying in the United States. While larger socioeconomic factors may cause difficulties and confusions among Chinese students in their everyday lives, one of the biggest challenges in the academic setting is different teaching styles in classroom (Huang & Brown, 2009). It has been reported that Professors at American universities complain about their Chinese students' ability to participate in class (Hathaway, 2011). Some of them had to make changes to their curriculum because of the

© Springer Nature Singapore Pte Ltd. 2020
B. Cheng et al., *The New Journey to the West*, Education in the Asia-Pacific
Region: Issues, Concerns and Prospects 53,
https://doi.org/10.1007/978-981-15-5588-6_9

increasing presence of Chinese students. For example, Professor Kent E. St. Pierre from the University of Delaware, in order to accommodate Chinese students, decided to weigh less on class participation so that their final grades would not be pulled down too much (Bartlett & Fischer, 2011).

Re-examining the Concept of Chinese Learner

Obviously, language barrier is part of the reason why Chinese students tend to have difficulty adjusting and participating in class, but the issue goes deeper than that. In the West, there is a common perception that students in the Confucius Heritage Culture (CHC) are passive learners who succumb themselves to a teacher-dominated learning environment and use rote learning memorizing vast amounts of information for test taking and as a result are lacking independent and critical thinking skills (Kim, 2007; Li, 2001; Zhao, 2013; Zhou, Lam, & Chan, 2012). These students are sometimes referred to as the "Chinese learners" (Chan & Rao, 2009; Li & Cortazzi, 2011; Watkins & Biggs, 1996, 2001), which means that "Chinese students in CHC classrooms who are influenced by Chinese belief systems, and particularly by Confucian values" (Chan & Rao, 2009, p. 4). CHC is a cultural system that encompasses multiple Asian nations and regions such as mainland China, Hong Kong, Taiwan, Singapore, Japan and Korea (Biggs, 1996), and thus the concept of "Chinese learner" has been expanded to "Asian learner" to reflect the broader influence of Confucian values and traditions.

There are both deficit and surplus views associated with the concept of Chinese learner, thus the so-called "paradox of the Chinese learner." On one hand, Chinese learners are often described as (1) a passive rote learner who relies heavily on memorization (Gow, Balla, Kember, & Hau, 1996; Li, 2009), (2) lacking critical thinking skills (Ryan, 2010), and (3) reluctant to speak up and ask questions in class discussion (Biggs, 1996; Wu, 2015). Further, the learning environment these learners were exposed to in Asia often seems to be unfavorable in Western standards: large class sizes, expository instructional styles, norm-referenced assessment (i.e., test-driven), and seemingly cold classroom environment (Biggs, 1996; Chan & Rao, 2009). On the other hand, however, the surplus view portrays CHC students as being cooperative, deep learners who are diligent, hard-working, and have a high regard for education (Chan & Rao, 2009; Ryan, 2010). It is also widely recognized that Chinese students are academically successful. For example, Chinese students are among the top performers on standardized international tests such as Program in Student Achievement (PISA) and Trends in International Mathematics and Science Study (TIMSS), and overseas Chinese students often perform better than their peers residing the same neighborhood (Gow et al., 1996).

Despite the increased interactions between the Western world and the CHC learners enabled by intensified internationalization of education, the paradox of Chinese learner continues to puzzle the Western world. Even Western educators who have taught Chinese students both in and outside China, and Western researchers who have observed these students from a distance tend to base their judgments of "the Chinese learner" largely on those stereotypical assumptions.

To what extent those stereotypical assumptions are true remains an important question. There are fundamental differences with regard to how a learner should act and how a learning process should unfold, and the stereotypical assumptions that Chinese students are rote learners and lack critical thinking skills are not well grounded. Holliday (1999) calls the above-mentioned deficit view of Chinese learner a "large culture" approach, which sees cultures "in their most typical form as geographically (and often nationally) distinct entities, relatively unchanging and homogeneous, and as all-encompassing systems of rules or norms that substantially determine personal behavior" (Clark & Gieve, 2006, p. 55; also see Atkinson, 1999).

The Issue of Rote Learning

First of all, the definition of rote learning does not conceptually fall in line with the CHC because for the CHC, learning by rote really means reflecting rather than a mere mindless act of repeating information (Dahlin & Watkins, 2000; Hay, 2007). In the Confucian tradition, memorization proceeds understanding and leads to deeper understanding (Lee, 1996), and evidence suggests that Chinese students combine memorization and understanding (Biggs, 1996; Gow, Balla, Kember, & Hau, 1996). The Western conception describes the practice of rote learning as surface memorizing without thought (Yu, 2013). The task for the CHC students, however, whether it is performing math problems or learning volumes of new information, involves a disciplined process of deep learning (Kennedy, 2002). In other words, memorization leads to understanding, and understanding can facilitate memorization, (Marton, Dall'Alba, & Tse, 1996). Li and Cutting (2011) call this "Active Confucian-Based Memory Strategies."

Second, unlike what has been commonly perceived in the West, the Chinese teacher with an authoritative manner does not necessarily hinder the learning process. In the CHC, the authority of the teacher is accepted, which facilitates productive learning both inside and outside the classroom (Watkins & Biggs, 2001). Further, Chinese students tend not to see authoritative teaching practices as controlling as American students do (Li, 2005; Zhou et al., 2012). Li (2005) reports that Chinese students believed in initially committing new material to memory and applying their understanding to real-life situations before approaching their teachers for answers. Li (2005) and Rosemont and Ames (2016) further clarify that the respect for teachers does not mean that students are blindly following, but rather are expressing their humility toward the student–teacher relationship.

Third, learning by heart and a teacher with authoritative manner may actually help to intrinsically motivate students to learn and at the same time foster students' independent and critical thinking skills. The values of learning in a CHC learning system focus on self-cultivation, and this self-cultivation involves perseverance and the process of enduring learning activities guided by teaching authorities (Li, 2005; Rosemont & Ames, 2016).

Similarly, Tan (2016) asks the question of whether good education must necessarily be learner-centered, as defined in the Western context (O'Neill & McMahon, 2005). Even though traditional Chinese teaching only satisfies one out of the three criteria of student-centered learning as students have a very low level of choice over the curriculum and the power resides primarily with the teacher, students are far from being passive learners. In fact, they are actively engaged in obtaining deep understanding and moral cultivation. Tan (2016) calls this approach "teacher-directed and learner-engaged" (p. 308) which challenges the assumption that good pedagogy has to be learner-centered.

The Issue of Critical Thinking

The definition of critical thinking has two dimensions, namely, the reasoning skills and critical spirit. The former refers to the capability for logic analysis and consistency, and the latter refers to the disposition to challenge and question existing dominant social and intellectual frameworks (Siegel, 1988; Walters, 1994).

According to Nussbaum (2017), what is crucial about course instruction is ample opportunity for interchange between faculty and students, many writing assignments, as well as feedback on assignments. Therefore, it is not necessarily discussion itself that is essential, but the interaction and feedback one may gain during the discussion. The common perception is that critical thinking is a Western construct and Chinese are lacking in critical thinking. However, what is considered good reasoning may not be universal (Lloyd, 1996; Moore, 2004). If critical thinking is equated with "logical analysis and argumentation that prevail in Western educational institutions" (Tan, 2017, p. 332), one may see a dearth of critical thinking in non-Western context. However, this definition of critical thinking is culturally biased and circular, according to Tan (2017). In her elaboration on the Confucian concepton of critical thinking, Tan (2017) defines critical thinking as "judgment" which is manifested in the "Confucian ideal of li" which require individuals to think and act "normatively, autonomously and judiciously in every situation" (p. 334). As Yang (2016) concludes: "It would be a serious error to assume that critical thinking is the preserve of Western cultures" (p. 29).

Contrary to the common stereotype that traditional Chinese way of teaching and learning does not foster independent and critical thinking, the Chinese pedagogic tradition helps to cultivate those skills and develop students' motivation to learn. An important pedagogic approach in the traditional Chinese way of learning is having students keep intellectual diaries of their readings which are regularly reviewed by their teachers and tutors.

Typically, in the diary of readings, the student wrote down what had been learned from the texts and also questions raised by the reading. The teacher/tutor would go over the diaries carefully with the student. They usually "reinforce astute observations the student had made on the texts, and corrected misunderstandings in the student's notes… [They were] vigilant in overseeing each student's diligence and depth of understanding" (Keenan, 1998, p. 40). This pedagogy not only fosters a close student–teacher relationship, but also enhances self-defined learning of the learner. In this learning process, students "had not only discovered this capacity [to learn] in themselves, and had thereby fostered their own self-confidence as independent learners for life" (Keenan, 1998, p. 42). In fact, as Zhao (2013) demonstrated through comparing Confucius' educational thought with that of such theorists in critical pedagogy as Paulo Freire and John Dewey, there are common threads between Confucian concepts of education and critical pedagogy, and Confucius is thus called "a critical educator."

The Need for a Purpose

Overcoming the stereotypical assumptions about the Chinese learner takes concerted efforts from both international students and their host societies. A fundamental issue in overcoming those barriers in understanding, however, calls for a shift in mindset as a common challenge faced by both the East and West is the lack of purpose in today's education. The purpose of education is not to compete or divide, but to unite, to collaborate, to improve understanding, and to make changes for the better, which, in other words, is to cultivate a Cosmopolitan spirit among students and citizens. Having a good understanding of this purpose not only helps with international students' adaptation, but can also contribute to building a more equitable and just world.

In addition to learning facts, mastering techniques such as reasoning, education means something more: "It means learning how to be a human being capable of love and imagination" (Nussbaum, 2017, p. 224). Without this "something more," students could only have what Harry R. Lewis, the former Dean of Harvard College, calls "excellence without a soul" (Lewis, 2006). They are merely what Williams Deresiewicz, who graduated from Columbia, and taught for a decade at Yale, calls "excellent sheep" (Deresieqicz, 2015).

With the deepening of the globalization process, boundaries between nations are fading, and nation-state is weakening as the principal site of identity construction. To the extent that there are anti-globalization movements and trends in some countries that try to reassert national identities, the cosmopolitan ideals and the ideal of global citizenship may be needed more than ever in a globalized world. As Rizvi (2009) states: "this new interest in cosmopolitanism is based upon a recognition that our world is increasingly interconnected and interdependent global, and that most of our problems are global in nature requiring global solutions" (p. 253). In this regard, education plays an important role in "connecting the *facts* of cosmopolitan encounters and the *values* that cosmopolitanism espouses" (Rizvi & Beech, 2017, p.126). In responding to the increasing global connectivity, Rizvi (2009) proposes a view of cosmopolitan learning, which is "a particular way of learning about our own social identities and cultural trajectories, but always in ways that underscore their connectivity with the rest of the world" (p. 264).

Becoming a cosmopolitan means being liberated from prejudice and isolation which can lead to loneliness and anxiety. Hansen (2010), the Columbia professor who has done extensive research on cultivating Cosmopolitan values through education, calls it a "cosmopolitan-minded education" which can "help people recognize …common features [of human life] as a renewed basis for mutual understanding and cooperation" (p. 2).

Cultivating Cosmopolitan Spirit

A sojourn refers to a "temporary stay" which could vary between 6 months and 5 years, and sojourners are those who "voluntarily go abroad for a set period of time that is usually associated with a specific assignment or contract" (Ward, Bochner, & Furnham, 2001, p. 21), and they are usually expected to return home after the completion of their assignment, contract, or studies. International students are one major group of international sojourners, and other groups include international business people, missionaries, and military personnel.

Research has shown that international sojourning such as education abroad can be a learning experience that results in growth in intercultural sensitivity and global competence (Campbell & Walta, 2015), and thus the development of cosmopolitan spirit and global citizenship (Braskamp, 2009; Davies & Pike, 2009). As Schattle (2008) argues, "traveling abroad to participate in educational programs has served a pivotal step in the lives of many self-described global citizens" (p. 15). Furnham and Bochner (1986) state that "sojourning makes a person more adaptable, flexible, and insightful" (p. 47). Similarly, Kim (2001) argues that "[d]espite, or rather because of, the difficulties crossing cultures entails, people do and must change some of their old ways so as to carry out their daily activities and achieve improved quality of life in the new environment" (p. 21). As Gu (2009) pithily summarizes: "when successful, intercultural experience can be a transformative learning process which leads to a journey of personal growth and development" (p. 40).

Of course, the transformation to global citizenship does not happen automatically through international travelling and sojourning. As Caruana (2014) states: "Encountering otherness abroad may involve rejection or narrow selection rather than openness, since the 'surrender' to openness is situational and dependent on the nature of intercultural contact" (p. 90). In fact, Allport (1979) argues that prejudice can only be reduced by intergroup contact that goes beyond the surface level and the groups involved enjoy equal status and common goals. Extensive research has been conducted since the original publication of Allport's influential intergroup contact theory in 1954. While the meta-analytic test of intergroup contact theory conducted by Pettigrew and Tropp (2006) largely supports Allport's conditions, conclusions regarding the effect of intergroup contact seem to be mixed and there are conflicting views. Even though there is still insufficient knowledge and understanding of how intercultural sensitivity and global competence are developed during the sojourn of international students (Savicki & Selby, 2008), Cheng and Yang (2019) reveal that international sojourning could potentially serve as an effective pathway to global citizenship because this type of sojourning may help international students develop relevant knowledge and understanding, skills, as well as values and attitudes through the mechanisms of non-vanity motives, a proactive mindset, exposure to different perspectives and experience with disadvantages.

International Sojourning as a Pathway to Cosmopolitanism

Every cosmopolitan argues for some community among all human beings, regardless of social and political affiliation (Kleingeld & Brown, 2013), and the main conception of cosmopolitanism is moral cosmopolitanism because of its strong emphasis on universal and cosmopolitan ethic (Delanty, 2006). But there are strong and weak conceptions of cosmopolitanism, as Delanty (2006) put it, or strict and moderate forms, as Kleingeld and Brown (2013) claim. The strict conception, represented by Nussbaum's liberal cosmopolitanism, emphasizes a firm commitment to universalism and requires some kind of exile of individuals from "the comfort of local truths, from the warm, nestling feeling of patriotism, from the absorbing drama of pride in oneself and one's own" (Nussbaum et al., 1996, p. 15). Appiah's rooted cosmopolitanism (Appiah, 2005), in comparison, adopts a more moderate approach and it acknowledges the importance of local context and local origins (Delanty, 2006; Tan, 2019).

It should be pointed out, though, that cosmopolitanism is not confined to western civilization. As Appiah (2008) argues: "this ideal [cosmopolitanism], or something very like it, was independently invented in other continents at other times" (p. 85). For example, the concept of ta t'ung, or the greater unity, in Confucianism refers to "the world commonwealth in which all men once strove for general welfare and harmony and which … should be restored" (Heater, 2004, p. 9), and it is quite similar to cosmopolitans' allegiance to the humankind.

Appiah (2005), in his defense of "rooted cosmopolitanism," states that cosmopolitans are people who construct their lives from whatever cultural resources to which they find themselves attached. Appiah's rooted cosmopolitanism is quite similar to Confucian cosmopolitanism which "calls for an expansion of family love to the world community so that universal harmony can be achieved" (Chen, 2016; Neville, 2012; Tan, 2019, p. 71), and his version of cosmopolitanism provides practical guidelines for how to implement cosmopolitanism in everyday life.

Appiah (2005) is not the only one who links cosmopolitanism with Confucianism. Ivanhoe (2014) provides two conceptions of Confucian cosmopolitanism. The first one is an ideal visitor or guest who "comes to another's country, temple, home, or life with an attitude of open curiosity, a characteristically Confucian 'love of learning,' and a desire for and anticipation of experiences that will deepen not only their knowledge about but appreciation of what it is to be human" (pp. 35–36). The other conception is cosmopolitanism as the attitudes of seeing other as part of one's family. This conception, however, does not require one to love strangers as much as one does siblings. As Ivanhoe (2014) states: "Confucian insists that our first and primary duties always remain focused on families. We extend our feelings beyond our families and out to those in the uttermost circle, but our love for them (our allegiance to them) is much less direct or intense" (p. 26).

Strict cosmopolitanism requires that we treat all members in the humanity equally. Love your neighbors as much as you do your family. In Confucian ethics, however, one would extend human compassion from one's family members and neighbors to "all within the Four Seas" (Mencius). As Mencius says: "Treat with the reverence due to age the elders in your own family, so that he elders in the families of others shall be similarly treated; treat with the kindness due to youth the young in your own family, so that the young in the families of others shall be similarly treated." The call for extending our love for family members to the world community is similar to Nussbaum's metaphor of "concentric circles" (Nussbaum et al., 1996, p. 9), where we will "see ourselves as existing in an innermost circle around which are larger and larger circles representing close family, friends, neighbors, fellow citizens, and ultimately everyone in the world" (Ivanhoe, 2014, p. 26). Her view, which calls on us to "treat strangers more like distant neighbors" however, is more demanding than Confucian cosmopolitanism which asks us to "treat strangers on the model of our family" (Ivanhoe, 2014, p. 27).

Concluding Remarks

While running the risk of increasing global inequality, transnational mobility also provides opportunities for people around the world to build solidarity and instill in them a cosmopolitan spirit. During the process of international sojourning, there is potential for students' knowledge to be enhanced as regards themselves and other cultures and their understanding of the common predicament and vulnerability of humanity, potential for their skills to be fostered in thinking, analyzing, and performing tasks, and potential for their values to be cultivated in open-mindedness, empathy, and compassion, respect for diversity and difference. As a result, they could be potentially better equipped for the challenges and hardships during the process of adaptation. Further, they could potentially develop concern for others, and the ability to relate to others, to feel others' pain and joy, and to understand the common predicament and vulnerability of humanity. Their life experiences may be greatly enriched and enhanced this way. A society full of citizens with cosmopolitan ideals would make it a more just and equitable, and thus better place to live in.

Just as intergroup contacts do not necessarily lead to reduced prejudice, international sojourning experiences do not necessarily lead to a higher level of global competencies or consciousness. It is the realization that all human beings share universal vulnerability and predicaments that ultimately makes one feel the affinity with humanity, and international sojourning experiences have the potential to wake up individuals to such a realization. As Rifkin (2010) states: "… the central human quality …was empathy for one another" (p. 8).

References

Allport, G. W. (1979). *The nature of prejudice (25th Anniversary Edition)*. Reading, MA: Addison-Wesley Publishing.

Appiah, K. A. (2005). *The ethics of identity*. Princeton, NJ: Princeton University Press.

Appiah, K. A. (2008). Education for global citizenship. In D. L. Coulter, J. R. Wiens, & G. D. Fenstermacher (Eds.), *Why do we educate? Renewing the conversation*. Wiley-Blackwell: Hoboken, NJ.

Atkinson, D. (1999). TESOL and culture. *TESOL Quarterly, 33*(4), 625–654.

Bartlett, T., & Fischer, K. (2011, November 3). The China conundrum: American colleges find the Chinese student boon a tricky fit. *The Chronicle of Higher Education*.

Biggs, J. B. (1996). Western misperceptions of the Confucian-heritage learning culture. In D. A. Watkins & J. B. Biggs (Eds.), *The Chinese learner: Cultural, psychological and contextual influences* (pp. 45–68). Hong Kong/Melbourne: Comparative Education Research Centre, the University of Hong Kong/Australian Council for Educational Research.

Braskamp, L. A. (2009). Internationalization in higher education: Four issues to consider. *Journal of College and Character, 10*(6), 1–7.

Campbell, C., & Walta, C. (2015). Maximising intercultural learning in short term international placements: Findings associated with orientation programs, guided reflection and immersion. *Australian Journal of Teacher Education, 40*(10), 1–15.

Caruana, V. (2014). Re-thinking global citizenship in higher education: From cosmopolitanism and international mobility to cosmopolitanisation, resilience and resilient thinking. *Higher Education Quarterly, 68*(1), 85–104.

Chan, C. K. K., & Rao, M. (2009). *Revisiting the Chinese learner: Changing contexts, changing education*. Hong Kong: Comparative Education Research Centre, the University of Hong Kong/Springer.

Chen, Y. (2016). Two roads to a world community: Comparing stoic and Confucian cosmopolitanism. *Chinese Political Science Review, 1*, 322–335.

Cheng, B., & Yang, P. (2019). Chinese students studying in American high schools: International sojourning as a pathway to global citizenship. *Cambridge Journal of Education, 49*(5), 553–573.

Clark, R., & Gieve, S. N. (2006). On the discursive construction of "The Chinese Learner". *Language, Culture, and Curriculum, 19*(1), 54–73.

Dahlin, B., & Watkins, D. (2000). The role of repetition in the processes of memorising and understanding: A comparison of the views of German and Chinese secondary school students in Hong Kong. *British Journal of Educational Psychology, 70*(1), 65–84.

Davies, I., & Pike, G. (2009). Global citizenship education: Challenges and possibilities. In R. Lewin (Ed.), *The handbook of practice and research in study abroad: Higher education and the quest for global citizenship* (pp. 61–78). New York, NY: Routledge.

Delanty, G. (2006). The cosmopolitan imagination: Critical cosmopolitanism and social theory. *The British Journal of Sociology, 57*(1), 25–47.

Deresieqicz, W. (2015). *Excellent sheep: The miseducaiton of the American elite and the way to a meaningful life*. New York: Free Press.

Furnham, A., & Bochner, S. (1986). *Culture shock: Psychological reactions to unfamiliar environments*. New York: Methuen.

Gow, L., Balla, J., Kember, D., & Hau, K. T. (1996). The learning approaches of Chinese people: A function of socialization processes and the context of learning? In M. H. Bond (Ed.), *The handbook of Chinese psychology* (pp. 109–123). Hong Kong: Oxford University Press.

Gu, Q. (2009). Maturity and interculturality: Chinese students' experiences in UK higher education. *European Journal of Education, 44*(1), 37–52.

Hansen, D. T. (2010). Cosmopolitanism and education: A view from the ground. *Teachers College Record, 112*(1), 1–39.

Hathaway, T. (2011, September 4). How American colleges can better serve Chinese applicants. *The Chronicle of Higher Education.*

Hay, D. B. (2007). Using concept maps to measure deep, surface and non-learning outcomes. *Studies in Higher Education, 32*(1), 39–57.

Heater, D. (2004). *Citizenship: The civic ideal in world history, politics and education.* Manchester: Manchester University Press.

Holliday, A. (1999). Small cultures. *Applied Linguistics, 20*(2), 237–264.

Huang, J., & Brown, K. (2009). Cultural factors affecting Chinese ESL students' academic learning. *Education, 129*(4), 643–653.

Huang, J., & Klinger, D. (2006). Chinese graduate students at North American universities: Learning challenges and coping strategies. *The Canadian and International Education Journal, 35*(2), 48–61.

Ivanhoe, P. J. (2014). Confucian cosmopolitanism. *Journal of Religious Ethics, 42*(1), 22–44.

Jiang, X. (2011, November 3). Selecting the right Chinese students. *The Chronicle of Higher Education.*

Keenan, B. (1998). Revitalizing liberal learning. *Change, 30*(6), 38–42.

Kennedy, P. (2002). Learning cultures and learning styles: Myth-understandings about adult (Hong Kong) Chinese learners. *International Journal of Lifelong Education, 21*(5), 430–445.

Kleingeld, P., & Brown, E. (2013). *Cosmopolitanism. Stanford encyclopedia of philosophy online.* Accessed July 2, 2019, from https://plato.stanford.edu/entries/cosmopolitanism/

Kim, K. H. (2007). Exploring the interactions between Asian culture (Confucianism) and creativity. *The Journal of Creative Behavior, 41*(1), 28–53.

Kim, Y. (2001). *Becoming intercultural: An integrative theory of communication and cross-cultural adaptation.* Thousand Oaks, CA: Sage Publications.

Lee, W. O. (1996). The cultural context for Chinese learners: Conceptions of learning in the Confucian tradition. In D. A. Watkins & J. B. Biggs (Eds.), *The Chinese learners: Cultural, psychological and contextual influences* (pp. 25–41). Hong Kong/Melbourne: Comparative Education Research Centre, the University of Hong Kong/Australian Council for Educational Research.

Lewis, H. R. (2006). *Excellence without a soul: Does liberal education have a future?* New York: PublicAffairs.

Li, J. (2001). Chinese conceptualization of learning. *Ethos, 29*(2), 111–137.

Li, J. (2005). Mind or virtue: Western and Chinese beliefs about learning. *Current Directions in Psychological Science, 14*(4), 190–194.

Li, J. (2009). Learning to self-perfect: Chinese beliefs about learning. In C. K. K. Chan & M. Rao (Eds.), *Revisiting the Chinese learner: Changing contexts, changing education* (pp. 35–69). Hong Kong: Comparative Education Research Centre, the University of Hong Kong/Springer.

Li, J., & Cortazzi, M. (2011). *Researching Chinese learners: Skills, perceptions, and intercultural adaptations.* London: Palgrave Macmillan.

Li, X., & Cutting, J. (2011). Rote learning in Chinese culture: Reflecting active Confucian-based memory strategies. In L. Jin & M. Cortazzi (Eds.), *Researching Chinese learners.* London: Palgrave Macmillan.

Lloyd, G. E. R. (1996). *Adversaries and authorities: Investigations into ancient Greek and Chinese science.* Cambridge: Cambridge University Press.

Marton, F., Dall'Alba, G. A., & Tse, L. K. (1996). Memorizing and understand: The keys to the paradox? In D. A. Watkins & J. B. Biggs (Eds.), *The Chinese learners: Cultural, psycho-*

logical and contextual influences (pp. 69–84). Hong Kong/Melbourne: Comparative Education Research Centre, the University of Hong Kong/Australian Council for Educational Research.

Moore, T. (2004). The critical thinking debate: How general are general thinking skills? *Higher Education Research and Development, 23*(1), 3–18.

Myles, J., Qian, J., & Cheng, L. (2002). International and new immigrant students' adaptations to the social and cultural life at a Canadian university. In S. Bond & C. Bowry (Eds.), *Connections and complexities: The internationalization of Canadian higher education* (Occasional papers in higher education) (Vol. 11). Winnipeg, Center for Research and Development in Higher Education.

Neville, R. C. (2012). Dimensions of contemporary Confucian cosmopolitanism. *Journal of Chinese Philosophy, 39*(4), 594–613.

Nussbaum, M. (2017). Education for citizenship in an era of global connection. In P. Marber & D. Araya (Eds.), *The evolution of liberal arts in the global age* (pp. 213–225). New York, NY: Routledge.

Nussbaum, M., et al. (1996). Patriotism and cosmopolitanism. In J. Cohen (Ed.), *For love of country: Debating the limits of patriotism*. Boson, MA: Beacon Press.

O'Neill, G., & McMahon, T. (2005). Student-centre learning: What does it mean for students and lecturers? In G. O'Neill, S. Moore, & B. McMullin (Eds.), *Emerging issues in the practice of university learning and teaching* (pp. 27–36). Dublin: AISHE.

Pettigrew, T. F., & Tropp, L. R. (2006). A meta-analytic test of intergroup contact theory. *Journal of Personality and Social Psychology, 90*(5), 751–783.

Rifkin, J. (2010). *The empathic civilization: The race to global consciousness in a world in crisis*. New York, NY: Jeremy P. Tarcher.

Rizvi, F. (2009). Towards cosmopolitan learning. *Discourse: Studies in the Cultural Politics of Education, 30*(3), 253–268.

Rizvi, F., & Beech, J. (2017). Global mobilities and the possibilities of a cosmopolitan curriculum. *Curriculum Inquiry, 47*(1), 125–134.

Rosemont Jr., H., & Ames, R. T. (2016). *Confucian role ethics: A moral vision for the 21st century?* (Vol. 5). Gottingen: Vandenhoeck & Ruprecht.

Ryan, J. (2010). "The Chinese learner": Misconceptions and realities. In J. Ryan & G. Slethaug (Eds.), *International education and the Chinese learner* (pp. 37–56). Hong Kong: Hong Kong University Press.

Savicki, V., & Selby, R. (2008). Synthesis and conclusions. In V. Savicki (Ed.), *Developing intercultural competences and transformation: Theory, research and application in international education*. Sterling, VA: Stylus.

Schattle, H. (2008). *The practices of global citizenship*. Lanham, MD: Rowman & Littlefield Publishers.

Siegel, H. (1988). *Educating reason: Rationality, critical thinking, and education* New York and London: Routledge.

Tan, C. (2016). Teacher-directed and learner-engaged: Exploring a Confucian conception of education. *Ethics and Education, 10*(3), 302–312.

Tan, C. (2017). A Confucian conception of critical thinking. *Journal of Philosophy of Education, 51*(1), 331–343.

Tan, C. (2019). Mencius' extension of moral feelings: Implications for cosmopolitan education. *Ethics and Education, 14*(1), 70–83.

Walters, K. (1994). Introduction: Beyond logicism in critical thinking. In K. Walters (Ed.), *Re-thinking reasons: New perspectives in critical thinking* (pp. 33–42). Albany, NY: SUNY Press.

Ward, C., Bochner, S., & Furnham, A. (2001). *The psychology of culture shock*. Philadelphia, PA: Routledge.

Watkins, D. A., & Biggs, J. B. (1996). *The Chinese learner: Cultural, psychological and contextual influences*. Hong Kong/Melbourne: Comparative Education Research Centre, the University of Hong Kong/Australian Council for Educational Research.

Watkins, D. A. & Biggs, J. B. (2001). *Teaching the Chinese learner: Psychological and pedagogical perspectives*. Hong Kong: Comparative Education Research Centre, the University of Hong Kong; Melbourne: The Australian Council for Educational Research Ltd.

Wu, Q. (2015). Re-examining the "Chinese learner": A case study of mainland Chinese students' learning experiences at British universities. *Higher Education, 70*, 753–766.

Yang, R. (2016). The East-West axis? Liberal arts education in East Asian universities. In I. Jung, M. Nishimura, & T. Sasao (Eds.), *Liberal arts education and colleges in East Asia: Possibilities and challenges in the global age* (pp. 27–37). Singapore: Springer.

Yu, X. (2013). Learning a foreign language through text and memorisation: The Chinese learners' perceptions. *Journal of Language Teaching and Research, 4*(4), 731–740.

Zhao, J. (2013). Confucius as a critical educator: Towards educational thoughts of Confucius. *Frontiers of Education in China, 8*(1), 9–27.

Zhou, N., Lam, S. F., & Chan, K. C. (2012). The Chinese classroom paradox: A cross-cultural comparison of teacher controlling behaviors. *Journal of Educational Psychology, 104*(4), 1–49.